# Mark A. Finley

# 10 Days in the UPPER ROOM

Pacific Press® Publishing Association
Nampa, Idaho
Oshawa, Ontario, Canada
www.pacificpress.com

Cover design by Steve Lanto
Cover resources from iStockphoto.com
Inside design by Aaron Troia
Inside resources from iStockphoto.com

Unless otherwise noted, scriptures are from The New King James Version, copyright © 1979, 1980, 1982, Thomas Nelson, Inc., Publishers.

The author assumes full responsibility for the accuracy of all facts and quotations as cited in this book.

You can obtain additional copies of this book by calling toll-free 1-800-765-6955 or by visiting http://www.adventistbookcenter.com.

Library of Congress Cataloging-in-Publication Data:

Finley, Mark, 1945-
Ten days in the Upper Room / Mark A. Finley.
    p. cm.
ISBN 13: 978-0-8163-2487-3 (pbk.)
ISBN 10: 0-8163-2487-5 (pbk.)
1. Pentecost.  2. Baptism in the Holy Spirit.  3. Spiritual life—
Seventh-day Adventists.  I. Title.
BT123.F57 2011
234'.13—dc22

                                        2011004170

12 13 14 15 • 5 4 3 2

# Contents

# Welcome

**W**elcome to an incredible spiritual journey to the Upper Room. Let me assure you that you are poised to make some of the most thrilling biblical discoveries of your life. During these studies, we will explore the preparation necessary to receive the Holy Spirit's power in all of its fullness. Together we will survey Inspiration's instructions on the reception of the Holy Spirit and on how to live daily in the power of the Spirit.

Have you ever wondered why the disciples had such death-defying faith? What gave them the courage to proclaim the gospel to the ends of the earth in spite of such overwhelming odds? Why were they so different after Pentecost? Peter's boastful claims were turned into submissive obedience and powerful proclamation. Thomas's doubts were transformed into rock-solid faith. James and John, the Sons of Thunder, were totally changed; they became humble servants of the Lord Jesus. Matthew, the cunning tax collector, became a faithful chronicler of the gospel; and Mary, a woman of ill repute, became a secure, loving champion of the Cross. Pentecost made a dramatic difference in their lives—and it can make a difference in our lives too. Filled with the power of the Holy Spirit, they changed the world. In just a few decades, the gospel was carried to the ends of the Roman Empire.

Is Jesus' promise of the Holy Spirit for these disciples alone? Is the outpouring of Heaven's power limited to them? Or, perhaps, does God have more for us, too, than we can possibly imagine? Speaking of Pentecost's promise, Peter declares, "The promise is to you and to your children, and to all who are afar off, as many as the Lord our God will call" (Acts 2:39).

Ellen White reaffirms that the gift is for us as well.

The lapse of time has wrought no change in Christ's parting promise to send the Holy

Spirit as His representative. It is not because of any restriction on the part of God that the riches of His grace do not flow earthward to men. If the fulfillment of the promise is not seen as it might be, it is because the promise is not appreciated as it should be. If all were willing, all would be filled with the Spirit. Wherever the need of the Holy Spirit is a matter little thought of, there is seen spiritual drought, spiritual darkness, spiritual declension and death. Whenever minor matters occupy the attention, the divine power which is necessary for the growth and prosperity of the church, and which would bring all other blessings in its train, is lacking, though offered in infinite plenitude (*The Acts of the Apostles,* p. 50).

> God longs to pour out the Holy Spirit upon His church today.

Both the Bible and the writings of the modern-day gift of prophecy clearly reveal that the promise of the Holy Spirit is for each one of us. God longs to pour out the Holy Spirit upon His church today. It is not because of any reluctance on the part of God that the Holy Spirit has not been poured out in latter-rain power for the finishing of God's work. All of Heaven waits for God's people to take the steps necessary to receive the power of the Holy Spirit to complete the gospel commission.

In this workbook, we will revisit the Upper Room and specifically study the preparation necessary to receive the outpouring of the Holy Spirit at the end time. Each chapter contains three distinct sections: Examining Divine Counsel, Reflecting on Divine Counsel, and Applying Divine Counsel. We will examine the disciples' heartfelt preparation before they received the Holy Spirit, reflect on the writings of both the Bible and Ellen White about the ministry of the Holy Spirit, and relate what we are learning from Inspiration to our lives as we fill out sections in the workbook. It is my prayer that as you study this material, you will be filled with the Holy Spirit in a life-transforming experience. I pray that God will empower you to be a mighty witness for Him at this decisive moment of earth's history.

> There in that Upper Room in Jerusalem, they prayed, repented of their sins, confessed their lack of faith, humbled their hearts, and surrendered their lives anew to the Holy Spirit's working.

## Why Pentecost is significant

The Day of Pentecost was extremely significant in Jewish history. Following fifty days after the Passover celebration, it commemorated both the spring harvest in Palestine's agricultural cycle and the giving of the law on Mount Sinai fifty days after the Exodus. For Christians, it commemorates the descent of the Holy Spirit. Some have called Pentecost "the birth of the Christian church." After His death and resurrection, Jesus appeared to the disciples for forty days (Acts 1:3). He commanded them to wait in Jerusalem to receive the promise of the mighty outpouring of the Holy Spirit as predicted in Joel 2:28. "It shall come to pass afterward that I shall pour out My Spirit on all flesh," the Savior declared. "You shall receive power when the

# Welcome

Holy Spirit has come upon you; and you shall be witnesses to me in Jerusalem, and in all Judea and Samaria, and to the end of the earth" (Acts 1:8).

Recognizing the significance of Christ's command, the disciples obeyed His instructions. There in that Upper Room in Jerusalem, they prayed, repented of their sins, confessed their lack of faith, humbled their hearts, and surrendered their lives anew to the Holy Spirit's working.

With divine insight, Ellen White describes what happened during their ten days together. "After Christ's ascension, the disciples were gathered together in one place to make humble supplication to God. And after ten days of heart searching and self-examination, the way was prepared for the Holy Spirit to enter the cleansed, consecrated soul temples" (*Evangelism*, p. 698).

> *The Christian church began its existence by praying for the Holy Spirit.*

The Christian church began its existence by praying for the Holy Spirit. It was in its infancy, without the personal presence of Christ. Just before His ascension Christ had commissioned the disciples to preach the gospel to the world. . . .

In obedience to the word of their Master the disciples returned to Jerusalem, and for ten days they prayed for the fulfillment of God's promise. These ten days were days of deep heart searching. The disciples put away all difference that had existed among them, and drew close together in Christian fellowship. . . . At the end of the ten days the Lord fulfilled His promise by a wonderful outpouring of His Spirit. When they were "all with one accord in one place" in prayer and supplication, the promised blessing came. . . .

What was the result of the outpouring of the Spirit on the day of Pentecost? The glad tidings of a risen Saviour were carried to the utmost bounds of the inhabited world. The hearts of the disciples were surcharged with benevolence so full, so deep, so far reaching, that it impelled them to go to the ends of the earth.

By the grace of Christ the apostles were made what they were. It was sincere devotion and humble, earnest prayer that brought them into close communion with Him. They sat together with Him in heavenly places. They realized the greatness of their debt to Him. By earnest, persevering prayer they obtained the endowment of the Holy Spirit, and then they went forth, weighted with the burden of saving souls, filled with zeal to extend the triumphs of the cross. . . .

> *The Great Commission is accompanied by the great promise. The task of preaching the gospel to the entire world in this generation may seem impossible, but God is the God of the impossible.*

Shall we be less earnest than were the apostles? Shall we not by living faith claim the promises that moved them to the depths of their being to call upon the Lord Jesus for the fulfillment of His word: "Ask, and ye shall receive" (John 16:24)? Is not the Spirit of God to come today in answer to earnest, persevering prayer, and fill men with power? (*In Heavenly Places*, p. 333).

*10 Days in the Upper Room* has been prepared in response

to this divine counsel. The Great Commission is accompanied by the great promise. The task of preaching the gospel to the entire world in this generation may seem impossible, but God is the God of the impossible. When the Holy Spirit is poured out in the fullness of His power, hearts will be touched, lives will be changed, and God's last-day message of truth will spread like wildfire. Our sons and daughters who have drifted from Jesus will come home. Backsliders will return to the God of their childhood. Hard hearts will be softened and closed minds opened. Countries resistant to the gospel will become fertile fields for the reception of God's truth. The earth will be "illuminated with . . . glory" (Revelation 18:1). The work of God on earth will be finished, and Jesus will come.

## Why God unleashed Heaven's power

Heaven's power was unleashed on Pentecost for two main reasons. First, the time was right. The Holy Spirit was poured out on the disciples as confirmation that Christ's sacrifice was accepted in heaven. He was now exalted as our Savior and Lord. Peter explained this in his sermon on Pentecost when he proclaimed, "Therefore being exalted to the right hand of God, and having received from the Father the promise of the Holy Spirit, He poured out this which you now see and hear" (Acts 2:33). The descent of the Holy Spirit was the divine signal that the disciples had a Friend at the throne of God who would daily empower them to accomplish His mission. The clock struck the hour in the divine timetable of heaven, and the Spirit was poured out with all power. "Christ determined to bestow a gift on those who had been with Him and on those who should believe on Him, because this was the occasion of His ascension and inauguration, a jubilee in heaven. What gift could Christ bestow rich enough to signalize and grace His ascension to the mediatorial throne? It must be worthy of His greatness and His royalty. Christ gave His representative, the third person of the Godhead, the Holy Spirit. This Gift could not be excelled" (*Christ Triumphant,* p. 301).

> The descent of the Holy Spirit was the divine signal that the disciples had a Friend at the throne of God who would daily empower them to accomplish His mission.

The second reason the Holy Spirit was poured out was that the disciples met the conditions. Something miraculous happened during those ten days in the Upper Room that prepared them to receive the Spirit in all of its fullness. In the first century, the disciples received the power of the Holy Spirit to launch the gospel message. God's end-time church will receive the fullness of the Spirit's power to complete the task of proclaiming the gospel to the world.

The time is right. The hour has come. Our Lord is appealing to His church today to meet the conditions. A careful study of both the Bible and the writings of Ellen White reveal the experience of the disciples during those ten days in the Upper Room. They sought for a renewed experience with God through the following activities:

1. Earnest intercession
2. Deeper faith
3. Heartfelt repentance

    4. Honest confession
    5. Loving unity
    6. Self-examination
    7. Sacrificial humility
    8. Obedient surrender
    9. Joyful thanksgiving
    10. Passionate witness

In the section "Examining Divine Counsel," we will study one of these character qualities in each chapter and ask these basic questions:

    1. How can I prepare my heart to receive the fullness of the Holy Spirit's power?
    2. Is there anything in my life that hinders the outpouring of the Holy Spirit?
    3. Can God safely trust me with the power of His Holy Spirit?
    4. Is my heart prepared to receive the promised latter rain?

As we study these topics together, you will sense yourself being drawn even closer to the Savior. As you daily open your heart to the Holy Spirit's influence, you will experience an even more intimate experience with Jesus. The power of the Spirit will fill your life anew. The baptism of the Holy Spirit is not something we seek once, nor is it some glorious experience we longingly wait for in the future. The infilling of the Holy Spirit is an experience we seek every day. "For the daily baptism of the Spirit every worker should offer his petition to God. Companies of Christian workers should gather to ask for special help, for heavenly wisdom, that they may know how to plan and execute wisely" (*The Acts of the Apostles,* p. 50).

May you experience the power of the Holy Spirit afresh in your life as you study these pages, and may your heart be open to receive everything that God has for His church today.

# Day 1

# Earnest Intercession

Prayer is the heartbeat of the disciples' ministry throughout their exploits of faith in the book of Acts. They gathered together for ten days and earnestly sought the promised Holy Spirit. After the Holy Spirit was poured out, in only one day three thousand new converts were added. "They continued steadfastly in the apostles' doctrine and fellowship, in the breaking of bread, and in prayers" (Acts 2:42). When facing overwhelming obstacles, the disciples appealed to their best Friend, Jesus, who stood at the right hand of God's throne, and "the place where they were assembled together was shaken; and they were all filled with the Holy Spirit, and they spoke the Word of God with boldness" (Acts 4:31). Soon the early church chose deacons so the apostles could give themselves "continually to prayer and to the ministry of the word" (Acts 6:4). When Herod imprisoned Peter, the entire church interceded, and the apostle was miraculously released from prison (Acts 12).

The prayer experience in the Upper Room launched a life of prayer for the disciples' entire ministry. Through prayer they developed trusting hearts. Through prayer they established an attitude of dependence on the Almighty. Through prayer they acknowledged their weakness and sought His strength. Through prayer they admitted their ignorance and sought His wisdom. The disciples openly recognized their limitations and cried out for His all-sufficient power. They recognized they could never reach the world with the gospel without the presence and power of the Holy Spirit working through them. Pentecost was the result of heartfelt intercession.

## Prayer: The channel of blessing

Through prayer we, too, open our hearts to everything Jesus has for us. We lay our souls bare to receive the fullness of His power. "Prayer is the opening of the heart to God as to a friend. Not that it is necessary in order to make known to God what we are, but in order to enable us to receive Him. Prayer does not bring God down to us, but brings us up to Him" (*Steps to Christ,* p. 93). In all healthy relationships there is the desire to communicate with the person we care about. Prayer opens our hearts to speak with God just like we would a close friend or companion. The Upper Room was a place of communion with God, a place where the disciples prayed individually and united in corporate prayer. They "met together to present their requests to the Father in the name of Jesus. They knew that they had a Representative in heaven, an Advocate at the throne of God. In solemn awe they bowed in prayer, repeating the assurance, 'Whatsoever ye shall ask the Father in My name, He will give it you. Hitherto have ye asked nothing in My name: ask, and ye shall receive, that your joy may be full.' John 16:23, 24. Higher and still higher they extended the hand of faith, with the mighty argument, 'It is Christ that died, yea rather, that is risen again, who is even at the right hand of God, who also maketh intercession for us.' Romans 8:24" (*The Acts of the Apostles,* pp. 35, 36).

> *Prayer opens our hearts to speak with God just like we would a close friend or companion.*

We, too, have a Representative in heaven who invites us to bring our burdens to Him. We have a Friend at the throne of God who urges us to present the longings of our hearts to Him. We, too, can claim His promises. We, too, can extend our hands of faith higher and higher. We, too, can ask Him to bestow Heaven's most priceless gift of the Holy Spirit upon us. He invites us to come to the throne now to claim these precious promises.

In the great controversy between good and evil, prayer is a mighty weapon to defeat the enemy. One of the fundamental principles in God's universe is freedom of choice. God will never coerce our will. He will never manipulate us into serving Him. Although He daily works in our lives, impressing us by His spirit to make right choices, His involvement in our lives is limited by our choices. When we kneel before Him in prayer, He respects our choice for Him to intervene in our lives more fully. His Spirit impresses and convicts us before we pray, but His Spirit will never fill us and empower us until we pray.

Prayerfully read the Scripture and Ellen G. White passages below. Claim them as your own. Present these divine promises to the Lord, believing that He will fulfill His Word.

## Divine promises

- "If you then, being evil, know how to give good gifts to your children, how much more will your heavenly Father give the Holy Spirit to those who ask Him!" (Luke 11:13).
- "I will pray the Father, and He will give you another Helper, that He may abide with you forever" (John 14:16).
- "The Helper, the Holy Spirit, whom the Father will send in my name, He will teach you all things, and bring to your remembrance all the things that I said to you" (John 14:26).

# Day 1: Earnest Intercession

- "Ask, and it will be given to you; seek, and you will find; knock, and it will be opened to you. For everyone who asks receives, and he who seeks finds, and to him who knocks it will be opened" (Matthew 7:7, 8).

- "Heaven is full of light and strength, and we can draw from it if we will. God is waiting to pour his blessing upon us as soon as we draw nigh to him and by living faith grasp his promises. He says that he is more willing to give his Holy Spirit to those that ask him than earthly parents are to give good gifts unto their children. Shall we take him at his word?" (*Historical Sketches,* p. 152).

- "The lapse of time has wrought no change in Christ's parting promise to send the Holy Spirit as His representative. It is not because of any restriction on the part of God that the riches of His grace do not flow earthward to men. If the fulfillment of the promise is not seen as it might be, it is because the promise is not appreciated as it should be. If all were willing, all would be filled with the Spirit. Wherever the need of the Holy Spirit is a matter little thought of, there is seen spiritual drought, spiritual darkness, spiritual declension and death. Whenever minor matters occupy the attention, the divine power which is necessary for the growth and prosperity of the church, and which would bring all other blessings in its train, is lacking, though offered in infinite plenitude" (*The Acts of the Apostles,* p. 50).

> We are living at a special time in human history. All of Heaven invites us to grasp the promises of the Almighty. God longs to do something special for His church now.

- "Morning by morning, as the heralds of the gospel kneel before the Lord and renew their vows of consecration to Him, He will grant them the presence of His Spirit, with its reviving, sanctifying power. As they go forth to the day's duties, they have the assurance that the unseen agency of the Holy Spirit enables them to be 'laborers together with God' " (*The Acts of the Apostles,* p. 56).

- "Near the close of earth's harvest, a special bestowal of spiritual grace is promised to prepare the church for the coming of the Son of man. This outpouring of the Spirit is likened to the falling of the latter rain; and it is for this added power that Christians are to send their petitions to the Lord of the harvest 'in the time of the latter rain.' In response, 'the Lord shall make bright clouds, and give them showers of rain.' 'He will cause to come down . . . the rain, the former rain, and the latter rain,' Zechariah 10:1; Joel 2:23" (*The Acts of the Apostles,* p. 55).

We are living at a special time in human history. All of Heaven invites us to grasp the promises of the Almighty. God longs to do something special for His church now. He invites us to seek Him with all of our hearts to receive the power of His Holy Spirit in the latter rain for the finishing of His work on earth. Will you prayerfully claim His promises? Will you encourage others to join you in praying for the outpouring of the Holy Spirit? Will you now reorder your priorities to spend more time with Jesus in prayer?

## Section 2: Reflecting on Divine Counsel

Thoughtfully read the following excerpt from *The Desire of Ages,* pages 668–671.

Before offering Himself as the sacrificial victim, Christ sought for the most essential and complete gift to bestow upon His followers, a gift that **[page 669]** would bring within their reach the boundless resources of grace. "I will pray the Father," He said, "and He shall give you another Comforter, that He may abide with you forever; even the Spirit of truth; whom the world cannot receive, because it seeth Him not, neither knoweth Him: but ye know Him; for He dwelleth with you, and shall be in you. I will not leave you orphans: I will come to you." John 14:16–18, margin.

Before this the Spirit had been in the world; from the very beginning of the work of redemption He had been moving upon men's hearts. But while Christ was on earth, the disciples had desired no other helper. Not until they were deprived of His presence would they feel their need of the Spirit, and then He would come.

The Holy Spirit is Christ's representative, but divested of the personality of humanity, and independent thereof. Cumbered with humanity, Christ could not be in every place personally. Therefore it was for their interest that He should go to the Father, and send the Spirit to be His successor on earth. No one could then have any advantage because of his location or his personal contact with Christ. By the Spirit the Saviour would be accessible to all. In this sense He would be nearer to them than if He had not ascended on high.

"He that loveth Me shall be loved of My Father, and I will love him, and will manifest Myself to him." Jesus read the future of His disciples. He saw one brought to the scaffold, one to the cross, one to exile among the lonely rocks of the sea, others to persecution and death. He encouraged them with the promise that in every trial He would be with them. That promise has lost none of its force. The Lord knows all about His faithful servants who for His sake are lying in prison or who are banished to lonely islands. He comforts them with His own presence. When for the truth's sake the believer stands at the bar of unrighteous tribunals, Christ stands by his side. All the reproaches that fall upon him, fall upon Christ. Christ is condemned over again in the person of His disciple. When one is incarcerated in prison walls, Christ ravishes the heart with His love. When one suffers death for His sake, Christ says, "I am He that liveth, and was dead; and, behold, I am alive forevermore, . . . and have the keys of hell and of death." Revelation 1:18. The life that is sacrificed for Me is preserved unto eternal glory.

At all times and in all places, in all sorrows and in all afflictions, when the outlook seems dark and the future perplexing, and we feel helpless and alone, the Comforter will be sent in answer to the prayer of **[page 670]** faith. Circumstances may separate us from every earthly friend; but no circumstance, no distance, can separate us from the heavenly Comforter. Wherever we are,

> *The Holy Spirit is Christ's representative, but divested of the personality of humanity, and independent thereof.*

wherever we may go, He is always at our right hand to support, sustain, uphold, and cheer.

The disciples still failed to understand Christ's words in their spiritual sense, and again He explained His meaning. By the Spirit, He said, He would manifest Himself to them. "The Comforter, which is the Holy Ghost, whom the Father will send in My name, He shall teach you all things." No more will you say, I cannot comprehend. No longer will you see through a glass, darkly. You shall "be able to comprehend with all saints what is the breadth, and length, and depth, and height; and to know the love of Christ, which passeth knowledge." Ephesians 3:18, 19.

The disciples were to bear witness to the life and work of Christ. Through their word He was to speak to all the people on the face of the earth. But in the humiliation and death of Christ they were to suffer great trial and disappointment. That after this experience their word might be accurate, Jesus promised that the Comforter should "bring all things to your remembrance, whatsoever I have said unto you."

"I have yet many things to say unto you," He continued, "but ye cannot bear them now. Howbeit when He, the Spirit of truth, is come, He will guide you into all truth: for He shall not speak of Himself; but whatsoever He shall hear, that shall He speak: and He will show you things to come. He shall glorify Me: for He shall receive of Mine, and shall show it unto you." Jesus had opened before His disciples a vast tract of truth. But it was most difficult for them to keep His lessons distinct from the traditions and maxims of the scribes and Pharisees. They had been educated to accept the teaching of the rabbis as the voice of God, and it still held a power over their minds, and molded their sentiments. Earthly ideas, temporal things, still had a large place in their thoughts. They did not understand the spiritual nature of Christ's kingdom, though He had so often explained it to them. Their minds had become confused. They did not comprehend the value of the scriptures Christ presented. Many of His lessons seemed almost lost upon them. Jesus saw that they did not lay hold of the real meaning of His words. He compassionately promised that the Holy Spirit should recall these sayings to their minds. And He had left unsaid many things that could not be comprehended by the disciples. These also would be opened to them by the Spirit. The Spirit was to quicken their **[page 671]** understanding, that they might have an appreciation of heavenly things. "When He, the Spirit of truth, is come," said Jesus, "He will guide you into all truth."

The Comforter is called "the Spirit of truth." His work is to define and maintain the truth. He first dwells in the heart as the Spirit of truth, and thus He becomes the Comforter. There is comfort and peace in the truth, but no real peace or comfort can be found in falsehood. It is through false theories and traditions that Satan gains his power over the mind. By directing men to false standards, he misshapes the character. Through the Scriptures the Holy Spirit speaks to the mind, and impresses truth upon the heart. Thus He exposes error, and expels it from the soul. It is by the Spirit of truth, working through the word of God, that Christ subdues His chosen people to Himself.

In describing to His disciples the office work of the Holy Spirit, Jesus sought to inspire them

> At all times and in all places, in all sorrows and in all afflictions, when the outlook seems dark and the future perplexing, and we feel helpless and alone, the Comforter will be sent in answer to the prayer of faith.

with the joy and hope that inspired His own heart. He rejoiced because of the abundant help He had provided for His church. The Holy Spirit was the highest of all gifts that He could solicit from His Father for the exaltation of His people. The Spirit was to be given as a regenerating agent, and without this the sacrifice of Christ would have been of no avail. The power of evil had been strengthening for centuries, and the submission of men to this satanic captivity was amazing. Sin could be resisted and overcome only through the mighty agency of the Third Person of the Godhead, who would come with no modified energy, but in the fullness of divine power. It is the Spirit that makes effectual what has been wrought out by the world's Redeemer. It is by the Spirit that the heart is made pure. Through the Spirit the believer becomes a partaker of the divine nature. Christ has given His Spirit as a divine power to overcome all hereditary and cultivated tendencies to evil, and to impress His own character upon His church.

Of the Spirit Jesus said, "He shall glorify Me." The Saviour came to glorify the Father by the demonstration of His love; so the Spirit was to glorify Christ by revealing His grace to the world. The very image of God is to be reproduced in humanity. The honor of God, the honor of Christ, is involved in the perfection of the character of His people.

"When He [the Spirit of truth] is come, He will reprove the world of sin, and of righteousness, and of judgment." The preaching of the word will be of no avail without the continual presence and aid of the Holy Spirit. This is the only effectual teacher of divine truth. Only **[page 672]** when the truth is accompanied to the heart by the Spirit will it quicken the conscience or transform the life. One might be able to present the letter of the word of God, he might be familiar with all its commands and promises; but unless the Holy Spirit sets home the truth, no souls will fall on the Rock and be broken. No amount of education, no advantages, however great, can make one a channel of light without the co-operation of the Spirit of God. The sowing of the gospel seed will not be a success unless the seed is quickened into life by the dew of heaven. Before one book of the New Testament was written, before one gospel sermon had been preached after Christ's ascension, the Holy Spirit came upon the praying apostles. Then the testimony of their enemies was, "Ye have filled Jerusalem with your doctrine." Acts 5:28.

> *Only when the truth is accompanied to the heart by the Spirit will it quicken the conscience or transform the life.*

Christ has promised the gift of the Holy Spirit to His church, and the promise belongs to us as much as to the first disciples. But like every other promise, it is given on conditions. There are many who believe and profess to claim the Lord's promise; they talk about Christ and about the Holy Spirit, yet receive no benefit. They do not surrender the soul to be guided and controlled by the divine agencies. We cannot use the Holy Spirit. The Spirit is to use us. Through the Spirit God works in His people "to will and to do of His good pleasure." Philippians 2:13. But many will not submit to this. They want to manage themselves. This is why they do not receive the heavenly gift. Only to those who wait humbly upon God, who watch for His guidance and grace, is the Spirit given. The power of God awaits their demand and reception. This promised blessing, claimed by faith, brings all other blessings in its train. It is given according to the riches of the grace of Christ, and He is ready to supply every soul according to the capacity to receive.

## Section 3: Applying Divine Counsel
### Meeting the Conditions

Just before He ascended to heaven, Jesus promised to send His disciples the gift of the Holy Spirit. Believing His promise, they entered into earnest intercession for the power of the Spirit in their own lives. They sought God in prayer for the promised gift.

For many Christians, the Holy Spirit is some sort of vague, indefinable force. He is the most misunderstood Member of the Godhead. In today's lesson, we will study Jesus' promise of the Spirit, the work of the Spirit, and the ministry of the Spirit in our lives.

As we understand the Holy Spirit's ministry more fully, we will long for the power of His presence in our lives. Understanding the Holy Spirit's ministry more clearly, we appreciate Him more, and more diligently seek for His powerful presence.

As we understand the Spirit's work better, our spiritual experience will deepen, and we will cry out for the infilling of the Spirit in the power of the latter rain.

1. What practical limitation did Jesus have while He was here on earth that the Holy Spirit would not have? What significant statement did Jesus make to His disciples about "going away"?

   Summarize Jesus' words recorded in John 16:7.

   _____

   _____

   _____

   _____

Read *The Desire of Ages,* page 669, paragraphs 2 and 3, to complete the sentences below.

"Cumbered with humanity, Christ _____

_____

_____

_____."

"By the Spirit _____

_____

_____

_____."

"He would be _____

_____

_____

_____."

2. How does the Holy Spirit enable us to face the trials, challenges, and disappointments of life? (See John 14:18, 26, 27; *The Desire of Ages,* page 699, last paragraph, and page 670, paragraph 1.)

_____

_____

_____

_____

The Holy Spirit is our ever-present Companion, Friend, and Helper. He strengthens us in trials, encourages us in disappointment, guides us in making decisions, and empowers us in resisting temptation.

The Holy Spirit is not limited by time or space. He can be in all places at all times. We cannot fully comprehend this divine mystery, but nevertheless it is true. Praise God! His presence through His Spirit is with us always.

3. List three reasons why Jesus describes the Holy Spirit as the "Spirit of truth" (See *The Desire of Ages,* page 670, and paragraph 1 of page 671.)

_____

_____

_____

_____

_____

_____

_____

4. What is the role (function of) the Holy Spirit in character development? (See *The Desire of Ages,* page 671, paragraph 2.)

_____

_____

_____

_____

5. What is the chief work of the Holy Spirit? (See John 16:13, 14; *The Desire of Ages,* page 671, last paragraph.)

_____

_____

_____

The Holy Spirit is Jesus' special gift to His church. Without the presence of Jesus in our lives through the Holy Spirit, we are powerless to face the enemy. The presence of the Holy Spirit brings joy, peace, power, and victory in our walk with God. Without the infilling of the Holy Spirit, our Christian lives are joyless and powerless. We live lives of frustrated defeat rather than confident hope. Will you, right now, open your heart to the ministry of the Holy Spirit and pray this simple prayer?

*Dear Jesus,*

*Today, I thank You for Your promise of the Holy Spirit. Too often, I have neglected thinking about and asking for His infilling in my own life. Too often, I have attempted to live the Christian life in my own strength rather than trusting in the power of the Holy Spirit for victory.*

*Just now I open my heart to You. I claim the promise of Your Holy Spirit. I repent of my lack of spiritual focus at times and of trusting in my own strength.*

*Believing that You will honor Your word right now, I accept the gift of the Holy Spirit. Thank You, Lord, for giving me Heaven's most precious gift.*

*In Jesus' name, amen.*

# Day 2

# Deeper Faith

The disciples before Pentecost were dramatically different from the disciples after Pentecost. Before Pentecost, their growing faith often faltered. After Pentecost, it was rock solid. The outpouring of the Holy Spirit strengthened the disciples to face the opposition that would come as they proclaimed Jesus' love and grace. Cowering in fear in the high priest's courtyard at the time of Jesus' arrest, Peter denied Him by cowardly uttering, "I do not know the Man" (Matthew 26:72). His fragile faith was weak and vacillating. But listen to a changed Peter on Pentecost powerfully proclaiming the Old Testament evidence that Jesus was the Messiah. Compare Peter's courtyard denial to his response after Pentecost when the Jewish authorities tried to silence his voice. He boldly declared, "We cannot but speak the things which we have seen and heard" (Acts 4:20). The indwelling of the fullness of the Holy Spirit made all the difference. In his own strength, Peter was no match for the cunning devices of the enemy. But in Jesus' strength, he was more than able to live a life empowered by the Holy Spirit. The apostle Paul describes the empowerment of the Holy Spirit this way: "That He would grant you, according to the riches of His glory, to be strengthened with might through His Spirit in the inner man" (Ephesians 3:16). Strengthened by the Spirit, faith-filled Peter was a changed man.

## Day 2: Deeper Faith

### *Faith* defined

Faith grasps the promise of the Holy Spirit as a divine reality. It believes Christ's promise to grant His Holy Spirit in abundant measure. Faith is itself a gift of God (Romans 12:3). "Faith that enables us to receive God's gifts is itself a gift, of which some measure is imparted to every human being. It grows as exercised in appropriating the word of God. In order to strengthen faith, we must often bring it in contact with the word" (*Education*, pp. 253, 254). As we behold Jesus through His Word, the Spirit who inspired the Word grows our faith (Romans 10:17).

> *Faith is trusting God— believing that He loves us and knows best what is for our good.*

Faith, in reality, is trust. "Faith is trusting God— believing that He loves us and knows best what is for our good. Thus, instead of our own, it leads us to choose His way. In place of our ignorance, faith accepts His wisdom; in place of our weakness, His strength; in place of our sinfulness, His righteousness. Our lives, ourselves, are already His; faith acknowledges His ownership and accepts its blessing. Truth, uprightness, purity, have been pointed out as secrets of life's success. It is faith that puts us in possession of these principles" (*Education*, p. 253). Faith is believing that He loves us and always has our best good in mind. Through faith the Holy Spirit leads us to grasp the magnitude of the gift of grace so freely offered on Calvary. Through faith we receive spiritual strength to resist the temptations of the evil one. Through faith we are empowered to witness. Through faith we are motivated to do whatever Jesus asks and to obey whatever He commands. Faith grasps the promises of God and believes that they are our own.

> *Our lives, ourselves, are already His; faith acknowledges His ownership and accepts its blessing.*

At Pentecost, "higher and still higher they [the disciples] extended the hand of faith," and "under the Holy Spirit's working even the weakest, by exercising faith in God, learned to improve their entrusted powers and to become sanctified, refined, and ennobled" (*The Acts of the Apostles*, pp. 36, 49, 50). This experience can be ours. The Holy Spirit longs to both deepen and increase our faith. Our faith grows in the context of a close relationship with Jesus.

### Three practical ways to increase your faith

1. Expect the Holy Spirit to grow your faith as you study God's Word. Approach your Bible study with a sense of expectation. Believe the Spirit who inspired the Bible is going to accomplish miraculous changes in your life as you persist in studying the Word (2 Peter 1:3, 4).

2. Apply the promises of God's Word to your life. To receive the benefit of Bible study, it must be applied to your life individually. Put yourself in the story. What lesson is the Holy Spirit revealing to you in the text of scripture? What insights for daily living is He revealing? What convictions is He bringing to your mind?

3. Act on the "measure of faith" that God has already placed in your heart. Look beyond

the current circumstances of your life to the blessings God has for you in the near future. If the Holy Spirit impresses you to do something, do it believing you will be richly rewarded as you act on His Word.

*Faith is ours to exercise, but joyful feeling and the blessing are God's to give. The grace of God comes to the soul through the channel of living faith, and that faith it is in our power to exercise.*

To deepen your own faith, read the promises below, and in Jesus' name, claim them as your own.

- "With men, this is impossible but with God all things are possible" (Matthew 19:26).
- "Let us therefore come boldly to the throne of grace, that we may obtain mercy and find grace to help in time of need" (Hebrews 4:16).
- "[Look] unto Jesus, the author and finisher of our faith" (Hebrews 12:2).
- "Now this is the confidence that we have in Him, that if we ask anything according to His will, He hears us" (1 John 5:14).
- "The Lord would have all His sons and daughters happy, peaceful, and obedient. Through the exercise of faith the believer comes into possession of these blessings. Through faith, every deficiency of character may be supplied, every defilement cleansed, every fault corrected, every excellence developed" (*The Acts of the Apostles*, p. 564).
- "I have frequently seen that the children of the Lord neglect prayer, especially secret prayer, altogether too much; that many do not exercise that faith which it is their privilege and duty to exercise, often waiting for that feeling which faith alone can bring. Feeling is not faith; the two are distinct. Faith is ours to exercise, but joyful feeling and the blessing are God's to give. The grace of God comes to the soul through the channel of living faith, and that faith it is in our power to exercise.

*Many people will confuse feelings for faith. They will look for a spiritual experience that stimulates their emotions and makes them feel good.*

"True faith lays hold of and claims the promised blessing before it is realized and felt. We must send up our petitions in faith within the second veil, and let our faith take hold of the promised blessing, and claim it as ours. We are then to believe that we receive the blessing, because our faith has hold of it, and according to the word it is ours. 'What things soever ye desire, when ye pray, believe that ye receive them, and ye shall have them.' Mark 11:24. Here is faith, naked faith, to believe that we receive the blessing, even before we realize it. When the promised blessing is realized and enjoyed, faith is swallowed up. But many suppose they have much faith when sharing largely of the Holy Spirit, and that they cannot have faith unless they feel the power of the Spirit. Such confound faith with the blessing that comes through faith.

"The very time to exercise faith is when we feel destitute of the Spirit. When thick clouds of darkness seem to hover over the mind, then is the time to let living faith pierce the darkness and scatter the clouds. True faith rests on the promises contained in the word of God, and those only who obey that word can claim its glorious promises" (*Christian Experience and Teachings of Ellen G. White*, pp. 126, 127).

### Faith in short supply

Evidently, this trusting relationship with God through His Word will be in short supply at the end time. Jesus asked, "When the Son of Man comes, will He really find faith on the earth?" (Luke 18:8). Many people will confuse feelings for faith. They will look for a spiritual experience that stimulates their emotions and makes them feel good. Others will fall into the opposite trap of cold formalism. In spite of some people's confusion, the Holy Spirit is guiding His church to a much deeper experience of faith than we could possibly imagine—an experience of total trust in God, confidence in His Word, and obedience to His will.

> The Holy Spirit is guiding His church to a much deeper experience of faith than we could possibly imagine—an experience of total trust in God, confidence in His Word, and obedience to His will.

Is it your wholehearted desire to live a life of trusting faith? Why not kneel and ask the Holy Spirit to deepen your faith and lead you to live such a life now?

## Section 2: Reflecting on Divine Counsel

Thoughtfully read the following excerpt from *The Desire of Ages,* pages 673–678.

Now Peter's voice is heard vehemently protesting, "Although all shall be offended, yet will not I." In the upper chamber he had declared, "I will lay down my life for Thy sake." Jesus had warned him that he would that very night deny his Saviour. Now Christ repeats the warning: "Verily I say unto thee, That this day, even in this night, before the cock crow twice, thou shalt deny Me thrice." But Peter only "spake the more vehemently, If I should die with Thee, I will not deny Thee in anywise. Likewise also said they all." Mark 14:29, 30, 31. In their self-confidence they denied the repeated statement of Him who knew. They were unprepared for the test; when temptation should overtake them, they would understand their own weakness.

> *Jesus looks with compassion on His disciples. He cannot save them from the trial, but He does not leave them comfortless.*

When Peter said he would follow his Lord to prison and to death, he meant it, every word of it; but he did not know himself. Hidden in his heart were elements of evil that circumstances would fan into life. Unless he was made conscious of his danger, these would prove his eternal ruin. The Saviour saw in him a self-love and assurance that would overbear even his love for Christ. Much of infirmity, of unmortified sin, carelessness of spirit, unsanctified temper, heedlessness in entering into temptation, had been revealed in his experience. Christ's solemn warning was a call to heart searching. Peter needed to distrust himself, and to have a deeper faith in Christ. Had he in humility received the warning, he would have appealed to the Shepherd of the flock to keep His sheep. When on the Sea of Galilee he was about to sink, he cried, "Lord, save me." Matthew 14:30. Then the hand of Christ was outstretched **[page 674]** to grasp his hand. So now if he had cried to Jesus, Save me from myself, he would have been kept. But Peter felt that he was distrusted, and he thought it cruel. He was already offended, and he became more persistent in his self-confidence.

Jesus looks with compassion on His disciples. He cannot save them from the trial, but He does not leave them comfortless. He assures them that He is to break the fetters of the tomb, and that His love for them will not fail. "After I am risen again," He says, "I will go before you into Galilee." Matthew 26:32. Before the denial, they have the assurance of forgiveness. After His death and resurrection, they knew that they were forgiven, and were dear to the heart of Christ.

Jesus and the disciples were on the way to Gethsemane, at the foot of Mount Olivet, a retired spot which He had often visited for meditation and prayer. The Saviour had been explaining to His disciples His mission to the world, and the spiritual relation to Him which they were to sustain. Now He illustrates the lesson. The moon is shining bright, and reveals to Him a flourishing grapevine. Drawing the attention of the disciples to it, He employs it as a symbol.

"I am the true Vine," He says. Instead of choosing the graceful palm, the lofty cedar, or the strong oak, Jesus takes the vine with its clinging tendrils to represent Himself. The palm tree, the cedar, and the oak stand alone. They require no support. But the vine entwines about the trellis, and thus climbs heavenward. So Christ in His humanity was [page 675] dependent upon divine power. "I can of Mine own self do nothing," He declared. John 5:30.

"I am the true Vine." The Jews had always regarded the vine as the most noble of plants, and a type of all that was powerful, excellent, and fruitful. Israel had been represented as a vine which God had planted in the Promised Land. The Jews based their hope of salvation on the fact of their connection with Israel. But Jesus says, I am the real Vine. Think not that through a connection with Israel you may become partakers of the life of God, and inheritors of His promise. Through Me alone is spiritual life received.

"I am the true Vine, and My Father is the husbandman." On the hills of Palestine our heavenly Father had planted this goodly Vine, and He Himself was the husbandman. Many were attracted by the beauty of this Vine, and declared its heavenly origin. But to the leaders in Israel it appeared as a root out of a dry ground. They took the plant, and bruised it, and trampled it under their unholy feet. Their thought was to destroy it forever. But the heavenly Husbandman never lost sight of His plant. After men thought they had killed it, He took it, and replanted it on the other side of the wall. The vine stock was to be no longer visible. It was hidden from the rude assaults of men. But the branches of the Vine hung over the wall. They were to represent the Vine. Through them grafts might still be united to the Vine. From them fruit has been obtained. There has been a harvest which the passers-by have plucked.

"I am the Vine, ye are the branches," Christ said to His disciples. Though He was about to be removed from them, their spiritual union with Him was to be unchanged. The connection of the branch with the vine, He said, represents the relation you are to sustain to Me. The scion is engrafted into the living vine, and fiber by fiber, vein by vein, it grows into the vine stock. The life of the vine becomes the life of the branch. So the soul dead in trespasses and sins receives life through connection with Christ. By faith in Him as a personal Saviour the union is formed. The sinner unites his weakness to Christ's strength, his emptiness to Christ's fullness, his frailty to Christ's enduring might. Then he has the mind of Christ. The humanity of Christ has touched our humanity, and our humanity has touched divinity. Thus through the agency of the Holy Spirit man becomes a partaker of the divine nature. He is accepted in the Beloved. [page 676] This union with Christ, once formed, must be maintained. Christ said, "Abide in Me, and I in you. As the branch cannot bear fruit of itself, except it abide in the vine; no more can ye, except ye abide in Me." This is no casual touch, no off-and-on connection. The branch becomes a part of the living vine. The communication of life, strength, and fruitfulness from the root to the branches is unobstructed and constant. Separated from the vine, the branch cannot live. No more, said Jesus, can you live apart from Me. The life you have received from Me can be preserved only by continual communion. Without Me you cannot overcome one sin, or resist one temptation.

"Abide in Me, and I in you." Abiding in Christ means a constant receiving of His Spirit, a life

> Thus through the agency of the Holy Spirit man becomes a partaker of the divine nature. He is accepted in the Beloved.

of unreserved surrender to His service. The channel of communication must be open continually between man and his God. As the vine branch constantly draws the sap from the living vine, so are we to cling to Jesus, and receive from Him by faith the strength and perfection of His own character.

The root sends its nourishment through the branch to the outermost twig. So Christ communicates the current of spiritual strength to every believer. So long as the soul is united to Christ, there is no danger that it will wither or decay.

The life of the vine will be manifest in fragrant fruit on the branches. "He that abideth in Me," said Jesus, "and I in him, the same bringeth forth much fruit: for without Me ye can do nothing." When we live by faith on the Son of God, the fruits of the Spirit will be seen in our lives; not one will be missing.

"My Father is the husbandman. Every branch in Me that beareth not fruit He taketh away." While the graft is outwardly united with the vine, there may be no vital connection. Then there will be no growth or fruitfulness. So there may be an apparent connection with Christ without a real union with Him by faith. A profession of religion places men in the church, but the character and conduct show whether they are in connection with Christ. If they bear no fruit, they are false branches. Their separation from Christ involves a ruin as complete as that represented by the dead branch. "If a man abide not in Me," said Christ, "he is cast forth as a branch, and is withered; and men gather them, and cast them into the fire, and they are burned."

> *Abiding in Christ means a constant receiving of His Spirit, a life of unreserved surrender to His service.*

"And every branch that beareth fruit, He purgeth [pruneth] it, that it may bring forth more fruit." From the chosen twelve who had followed **[page 677]** Jesus, one as a withered branch was about to be taken away; the rest were to pass under the pruning knife of bitter trial. Jesus with solemn tenderness explained the purpose of the husbandman. The pruning will cause pain, but it is the Father who applies the knife. He works with no wanton hand or indifferent heart. There are branches trailing upon the ground; these must be cut loose from the earthly supports to which their tendrils are fastening. They are to reach heavenward, and find their support in God. The excessive foliage that draws away the life current from the fruit must be pruned off. The overgrowth must be cut out, to give room for the healing beams of the Sun of Righteousness. The husbandman prunes away the harmful growth, that the fruit may be richer and more abundant.

"Herein is My Father glorified," said Jesus, "that ye bear much fruit." God desires to manifest through you the holiness, the benevolence, the compassion, of His own character. Yet the Saviour does not bid the disciples labor to bear fruit. He tells them to abide in Him. "If ye abide in Me," He says, "and My words abide in you, ye shall ask what ye will, and it shall be done unto you." It is through the word that Christ abides in His followers. This is the same vital union that is represented by eating His flesh and drinking His blood. The words of Christ are spirit and life. Receiving them, you receive the life of the Vine. You live "by every word that proceedeth out of the mouth of God." Matthew 4:4. The life of Christ in you produces the same fruits as in Him. Living in Christ, adhering to Christ, supported by Christ, drawing nourishment from Christ, you bear fruit after the similitude of Christ.

# Section 3: Applying Divine Counsel
## Meeting the Conditions

The Holy Spirit witnesses of Jesus. If we surrender to His guidance, He will lead us into a closer relationship with our Lord. The Spirit reveals the matchless charms of Christ. He leads us to rest in His love, trust His guidance, and surrender to His will moment by moment. Jesus called this "abiding in Me." This experience of abiding in Christ deepens our faith. At Pentecost the disciples learned what it means to truly abide in Christ. In this lesson we, too, will discover what it means to daily "abide in Christ."

1. What is the essential difference between Peter before the Cross and Peter at Pentecost? Read *The Desire of Ages,* pages 672, 673, and compare with Acts 2:37–39, Acts 4:8–12, and Acts 5:29–32.

   _____

   _____

   _____

   _____

Spend a moment reflecting on things in your life that may need the cleansing grace of Christ. What has the Holy Spirit been convicting you of recently? Is He pointing out some cherished sin He longs for you to surrender? Prayerfully read Psalm 51 on your knees and ask God to do a deep work of the Holy Spirit in your heart.

2. Read John 15:1–8 and compare it with *The Desire of Ages,* page 675, paragraph 2. What is it about the symbolism of a vine that makes it an attractive and meaningful symbol of Jesus?

   _____

   _____

   _____

   _____

3. What does it mean to "abide in Christ"? (See *The Desire of Ages,* page 676.)

   _____

   _____

   _____

   _____

4. How does the Master Husbandman produce vines with the maximum amount of fruit? How does this relate to our own Christian experience? (See John 15:5 and *The Desire of Ages,* pages 676 and 677.)

_____

_____

_____

_____

5. How can we glorify God in our own personal lives? (See John 15:8 and *The Desire of Ages,* page 677, paragraph 1.)

_____

_____

_____

_____

The Holy Spirit convicts us of sin. He reveals hidden attitudes and dispositional traits we may be unaware of. Our loving Lord longs for each one of us to manifest the grace of His character. As we are willing to confront our faults and surrender them to Jesus, the Holy Spirit will empower us to live godly lives. Our faith will increase as we see the Holy Spirit working miracles in our own lives. The disciples' testimony after Pentecost was the testimony of how Jesus, through the power of the Holy Spirit, changed their lives. He did it for them, and if we allow Him to, He will do the same for us.

# Day 3
# Heartfelt Repentance

Just before His ascension, Jesus gave the disciples very specific instruction to "wait for the Promise of the Father" (Acts 1:4). What did He mean? Were they simply to sit idly in the Upper Room doing nothing—or did they have a distinct role to play in preparing their hearts to receive the heavenly gift? Were there some things they needed to do? If so, what were they? And most important, what can we learn about the outpouring of the Holy Spirit from their Upper Room experience?

Commenting on these ten days of waiting, with divine insight Ellen White gives us this valuable perspective: "After Christ's ascension, the disciples were gathered together in one place to make humble supplication to God. And after ten days of heart searching and self-examination, the way was prepared for the Holy Spirit to enter the cleansed, consecrated soul temples" (*Evangelism*, p. 698). In the powerful chapter "Pentecost," she adds, "As the disciples waited for the fulfillment of the promise, they humbled their hearts in true repentance and confessed their unbelief" (*The Acts of the Apostles*, p. 36).

> The Savior died for their self-inflated egos, their desire for preeminence, their pride, and their hardness of heart.

What did they have to repent of? I can imagine that there was quite a bit. James and John probably repented of their impatience and pride. Peter likely repented of his lack of faith and

> We can no more repent without the Spirit of Christ to awaken the conscience than we can be pardoned without Christ.

Thomas, of his doubt. All of the disciples knelt before God and laid bare their souls. They recognized that it was for their sins that Jesus was nailed to that cruel tree. The Savior died for their self-inflated egos, their desire for preeminence, their pride, and their hardness of heart. The Holy Spirit brought these praying disciples to a deep conviction of their sinfulness. In genuine repentance, no excuse is made for sin because it is "the goodness of God" that leads each one of us to repentance (Romans 2:4).

It is impossible to genuinely repent of our sins unless Jesus gives us the gift of repentance. In Acts 5, the apostles proclaim the Jesus whom "God has exalted to His right hand to be Prince and Savior, to give repentance to Israel and forgiveness of sins" (verse 31). Ellen White reminds us that "we can no more repent without the Spirit of Christ to awaken the conscience than we can be pardoned without Christ.

"Christ is the source of every right impulse. He is the only one that can implant in the heart enmity against sin. Every desire for truth and purity, every conviction of our own sinfulness, is evidence that His Spirit is moving upon our hearts" (*Steps to Christ,* p. 26).

### *Repentance* defined

Repentance is an attitude of deep sorrow for sin. We do not want to hurt the One who loves us so much by our sinful actions, attitudes, and choices. Recognizing His enormous love for us, we turn in abhorrence from anything that grieves Him in any way. But repentance involves even more than turning away from sin. It involves a change of heart.

> Repentance involves even more than turning away from sin. It involves a change of heart.

Things we once enjoyed, we now loathe. With David we cry out, "Create in me a clean heart, O God, and renew a steadfast spirit within me. Do not cast me away from Your presence, and do not take Your Holy Spirit from me" (Psalm 51:10, 11). The truly repentant heart longs to please Jesus in every aspect of life.

Throughout the book of Acts, repentance and the reception of the Holy Spirit are closely linked. At the conclusion of his sermon on Pentecost, Peter admonished his hearers to "repent and let every one of you be baptized in the name of Jesus Christ for the remission of sins; and you shall receive the gift of the Holy Spirit" (Acts 2:38). In Acts 3:19, he appeals to us, as well as his immediate audience, to "repent therefore and be converted, that your sins may be blotted out, so that times of refreshing may come from the presence of the Lord." Ellen White defines this refreshing from the presence of the Lord as the latter rain (*Early Writings,* p. 86). As we enter into repentance—a deep heartfelt sorrow for sin—God prepares our hearts for the reception of the Holy Spirit.

# Day 3: Heartfelt Repentance

## A summary of what we have learned about repentance

1. Repentance is a deep heart sorrow for sin that leads us to long to please Jesus in every area of our lives.
2. Repentance is a gift of God. Without the Holy Spirit's working in our lives to lead us to repent, it is impossible to experience genuine repentance.
3. Repentance involves not only a change in our actions but also a deep change in our attitudes.
4. Repentance prepares our hearts for the indwelling of the Holy Spirit.
5. Repentance is necessary to receive the latter rain and be mighty witnesses for Jesus in the final generation.

Are there things in your life that the Holy Spirit is convicting you of that are not in harmony with God's will? Do you have certain attitudes that are not like Jesus' attitudes? Do you knowingly cling to habits that need to be surrendered? Where is our Lord leading your life? What steps is He directing you to take? Are you willing to humble yourself before God in heartfelt repentance and ask Him to forgive you for your sinful attitudes?

> As we enter into repentance—a deep heartfelt sorrow for sin—God prepares our hearts for the reception of the Holy Spirit.

Laodicea, the church of the judgment hour, is pictured in Revelation as filled with spiritual pride. She claims to be rich and increased with goods and in need of nothing. God strips aside her pretense and hypocrisy, declaring that she is lukewarm and complacent, and He counsels her to "be zealous and repent" (Revelation 3:19).

Do you hear the Holy Spirit speaking to your heart? Why not fall on your knees and repent? Tell God you are not all you want to be. Ask Him to reveal hidden areas lurking deep inside that are not in harmony with His will. Surrender the things He points out to you. As you respond to the Spirit's appeals and fall on your knees in sorrow for your sin, God will fill your heart with the fullness of His Spirit.

## Section 2: Reflecting on Divine Counsel

Thoughtfully read the following excerpt from *The Acts of the Apostles,* pages 35–38.

As the disciples returned from Olivet to Jerusalem, the people looked on them, expecting to see on their faces expressions of sorrow, confusion, and defeat; but they saw there gladness and triumph. The disciples did not now mourn over disappointed hopes. They had seen the risen Saviour, and the words of His parting promise echoed constantly in their ears.

In obedience to Christ's command, they waited in Jerusalem for the promise of the Father—the outpouring of the Spirit. They did not wait in idleness. The record says that they were "continually in the temple, praising and blessing God." Luke 24:53. They also met together to present their requests to the Father in the name of Jesus. They knew that they had a Representative in heaven, an Advocate at the throne of God. In solemn awe they bowed in prayer, repeating the assurance, "Whatsoever ye shall **[page 36]** ask the Father in My name, He will give it you. Hitherto have ye asked nothing in My name: ask, and ye shall receive, that your joy may be full." John 16:23, 24. Higher and still higher they extended the hand of faith, with the mighty argument, "It is Christ that died, yea rather, that is risen again, who is even at the right hand of God, who also maketh intercession for us." Romans 8:34.

As the disciples waited for the fulfillment of the promise, they humbled their hearts in true repentance and confessed their unbelief. As they called to remembrance the words that Christ had spoken to them before His death they understood more fully their meaning. Truths which had passed from their memory were again brought to their minds, and these they repeated to one another. They reproached themselves for their misapprehension of the Saviour. Like a procession, scene after scene of His wonderful life passed before them. As they meditated upon His pure, holy life they felt that no toil would be too hard, no sacrifice too great, if only they could bear witness in their lives to the loveliness of Christ's character. Oh, if they could but have the past three years to live over, they thought, how differently they would act! If they could only see the Master again, how earnestly they would strive to show Him how deeply they loved Him, and how sincerely they sorrowed for having ever grieved Him by a word or an act of unbelief! But they were comforted by the thought that they were forgiven. And they determined that, so

> *As they meditated upon His pure, holy life they felt that no toil would be too hard, no sacrifice too great, if only they could bear witness in their lives to the loveliness of Christ's character.*

> *They determined that, so far as possible, they would atone for their unbelief by bravely confessing Him before the world.*

# Day 3: Heartfelt Repentance

far as possible, they would atone for their unbelief by bravely confessing Him before the world. [page 37] The disciples prayed with intense earnestness for a fitness to meet men and in their daily intercourse to speak words that would lead sinners to Christ. Putting away all differences, all desire for the supremacy, they came close together in Christian fellowship. They drew nearer and nearer to God, and as they did this they realized what a privilege had been theirs in being permitted to associate so closely with Christ. Sadness filled their hearts as they thought of how many times they had grieved Him by their slowness of comprehension, their failure to understand the lessons that, for their good, He was trying to teach them.

> They did not ask for a blessing for themselves merely. They were weighted with the burden of the salvation of souls.

These days of preparation were days of deep heart searching. The disciples felt their spiritual need and cried to the Lord for the holy unction that was to fit them for the work of soul saving. They did not ask for a blessing for themselves merely. They were weighted with the burden of the salvation of souls. They realized that the gospel was to be carried to the world, and they claimed the power that Christ had promised.

During the patriarchal age the influence of the Holy Spirit had often been revealed in a marked manner, but never in its fullness. Now, in obedience to the word of the Saviour, the disciples offered their supplications for this gift, and in heaven Christ added His intercession. He claimed the gift of the Spirit, that He might pour it upon His people.

"And when the Day of Pentecost was fully come, they were all with one accord in one place. And suddenly there came a sound from heaven as of a rushing mighty wind, and it filled all the house where they were sitting." [page 38] The Spirit came upon the waiting, praying disciples with a fullness that reached every heart. The Infinite One revealed Himself in power to His church. It was as if for ages this influence had been held in restraint, and now Heaven rejoiced in being able to pour out upon the church the riches of the Spirit's grace. And under the influence of the Spirit, words of penitence and confession mingled with songs of praise for sins forgiven. Words of thanksgiving and of prophecy were heard. All heaven bent low to behold and to adore the

> All heaven bent low to behold and to adore the wisdom of matchless, incomprehensible love.

wisdom of matchless, incomprehensible love. Lost in wonder, the apostles exclaimed, "Herein is love." They grasped the imparted gift. And what followed? The sword of the Spirit, newly edged with power and bathed in the lightnings of heaven, cut its way through unbelief. Thousands were converted in a day.

## Section 3: Applying Divine Counsel
### Meeting the Conditions

Filled with a sense of hope and expectation, the disciples gathered in the Upper Room. They had absolute confidence that Christ would fulfill His word. With humble hearts they repented for their lack of faith. They knew that as they met the conditions, the Holy Spirit would descend in mighty power.

1. What was the disciples' reaction to Christ's ascension? Why did this reaction surprise the crowds in Jerusalem? (See Luke 24:50–53 and *The Acts of the Apostles,* page 35, paragraph 1.)

   _____

   _____

   _____

2. Why were the disciples filled with such hope and confidence shortly after Christ's ascension? (See Acts 1:1–4 and *The Acts of the Apostles,* page 35, paragraph 2.)

   _____

   _____

   _____

The disciples believed Jesus' word. They claimed His promise. They obeyed His command. They waited in the Upper Room, earnestly seeking the outpouring of the Holy Spirit. In solemn awe they bowed in prayer, repeating the assurance, "Whatever you ask the Father in My name He will give you. Until now you have asked nothing in My name. Ask, and you will receive, that your joy may be full" (John 16:23, 24).

3. As the disciples waited for the fulfillment of Jesus' promise, what five very specific things did they do? (See *The Acts of the Apostles,* pages 36, 37.)

   A. _____

   _____

   B. _____

   _____

   C. _____

   _____

   D. _____

   _____

E. _____

_____

4. What was God's ultimate purpose in empowering His disciples with the outpouring of the Holy Spirit? (See Acts 1:8 and *The Acts of the Apostles,* page 37, paragraph 2.)

_____

_____

_____

5. What difference did the outpouring of the Holy Spirit on the Day of Pentecost make in the disciples' individual lives? (See *The Acts of the Apostles,* page 38, paragraph 1.)

_____

_____

_____

God longs to do something in us so that He can do something through us. He longs to do something for us so He can do something with us. He longs to transform our characters so He can empower our witness. What we are is more important than what we do. You can "do" without "being" but you can never "be" without "doing." Transformed characters lead to active witness and service. Why not open your heart to Jesus right now and ask Him to reveal His character in your life?

> What we are is more important than what we do. You can "do" without "being" but you can never "be" without "doing."

# Day 4

# Honest Confession

Confession of sin has always characterized genuine revival. Confession opens the heart and clears the way for the mighty outpouring of God's Spirit. If the channels of the soul are clogged by sin, the Spirit cannot flow through us to impact the world. Unconfessed sin becomes a hindrance to all that God desires to do through His church. The wise man states, "He who covers his sins will not prosper, but whosoever confesses and forsakes them will have mercy" (Proverbs 28:13). We will not "prosper" spiritually unless we are honest with ourselves and God. Unconfessed sin is a cancer of the soul. Before the Holy Spirit fills us and empowers us, He convicts us and instructs us. Unless we confess the sins the Holy Spirit points out, our hearts will become barren. If we refuse to listen to the voice of conviction, we will never receive the outpouring of the Holy Spirit in latter rain power.

> The rich treasures of heaven were poured out to them after they had searched their own hearts diligently and had sacrificed every idol.

As the disciples met in the Upper Room, earnestly seeking God in prayer, they clearly understood the need to honestly confess their sins to God and, where appropriate, to one another. "After the ascension of Christ, the Holy Spirit did not immediately descend. There were ten days after His ascension before the Holy Spirit was given. This time was devoted by the disciples to most earnest preparation for receiving so precious an endowment. The rich treasures of heaven were poured out to them after they had searched their own hearts diligently and had sacrificed every idol. They were before God, humbling their souls, strengthening their faith, confessing their sins" (*This Day With God,* p. 10). Previous to the outpouring of the Holy Spirit, a work of preparation was needed. "As the disciples waited for the fulfillment of the promise, they humbled their hearts in true repentance and confessed their unbelief" (*The Acts of the Apostles,* p. 36). If Christ's own disciples needed to prepare their hearts for the early rain to launch the gospel proclamation in Pentecostal power, how much more do we need to prepare our hearts today in earth's final climactic hour? If they needed to spend time in prayer, meditation, repentance, and confession, we need it much more. If sin blocked the way of the mighty outpouring of the Holy Spirit then, it certainly will do the same now. If confession prepared their hearts to receive the Holy Spirit, it will prepare our hearts as well.

> *If Christ's own disciples needed to prepare their hearts for the early rain to launch the gospel proclamation in Pentecostal power, how much more do we need to prepare our hearts today in earth's final climactic hour?*

## Confessing specific sins

The sanctuary service in the Old Testament provides a vital lesson in the nature of confession. When Israelites sensed the guilt of their sins and brought their offerings to the sanctuary, Leviticus 5 describes what happened next. "It shall be, when he is guilty in any of these matters, that he shall confess that he has sinned in that thing" (Leviticus 5:5). Confession was always very specific. The sinner who brought the lamb placed his hands upon the head of the sacrifice and confessed the very thing he had sinned. Commenting on the importance of confession, Ellen White states, "True confession is always of a specific character, and acknowledges particular sins. They may be of such a nature as to be brought before God only; they may be wrongs that should be confessed to individuals who have suffered injury through them; or they may be of a public character, and should then be as publicly confessed. But all confession should be definite and to the point, acknowledging the very sins of which you are guilty" (*Steps to Christ,* p. 38).

> *Sin clogs the arteries of our spiritual hearts. It corrodes the channels of the soul. It blocks the blessing God longs to pour out through us.*

Have you harbored critical thoughts? Have you spoken stinging hurtful words? Have you been impatient or unkind? Have you been lax in keeping the Sabbath or unfaithful in returning tithe? Sin clogs the arteries of our spiritual hearts. It corrodes the channels of the soul. It blocks the blessing God longs to pour out through us. The answer is confession. As we kneel before our forgiving and merciful God, confessing the specific sins the Holy Spirit convicts us of, we will receive forgiveness, freedom from guilt, and pardon. This leads us to two vital questions. When should we ask forgiveness from someone we have wronged? When is it appropriate to publically confess our sins?

## Confessing to God and to others

When should we confess our sins to God alone? The apostle Paul longed to have a "conscience without offense toward God and men" (Acts 24:16). We can have a clear conscience as we confess our sins to God. If after we have confessed to God, our sense of guilt still persists, we may want to ask ourselves this question: Have we wronged others or hurt them in any way that the Holy Spirit is leading us to ask their forgiveness? If we have argued with or become impatient or angry with another person, the Holy Spirit convicts us to ask his or her forgiveness. Here is an all-important principle when determining if we should ask forgiveness of another person. You repair the fence where it is broken. If your actions have created a rift in a relationship with another individual, asking their forgiveness can mend that broken fence in the relationship and testify of the power of God's grace working in your life. If you have spoken unkind words about someone, repair the fence where it is broken. Go to the person you have spoken to and attempt to repair the damage you have caused to another's reputation.

> *You repair the fence where it is broken.*

When is public confession appropriate? Only when the sins you have committed are public. If you have disavowed your commitment to Christ and brought public rebuke on His name and the name of His church, public confession is at times appropriate. Although it is certainly not necessary and extremely unwise to go into all of the lurid details of sin, a testimony of His grace and our sorrow for disappointing Him brings healing to our own hearts and to the church.

Jesus is still the pardoning, forgiving Savior. He still cleanses us from the guilt and shame of sin. When we come and honestly confess our sins to Him, our hearts are prepared to receive the indwelling of His Holy Spirit. To assist you in receiving the indwelling of the Holy Spirit, on your knees, pray through this series of questions:

1. Is there anything in my life that hinders me from receiving the outpouring of the Holy Spirit?
2. Is there some sin lurking deep within that I have not yet confessed and forsaken?
3. Is there someone I have hurt or offended whose forgiveness I should ask?
4. Have I fully accepted God's forgiveness, or do I still unnecessarily harbor feelings of guilt?
5. Do I fully trust Jesus to forgive my sins?

# Section 2: Reflecting on Divine Counsel

Thoughtfully read the following excerpt from *The Acts of the Apostles,* pages 38–45.

The Spirit came upon the waiting, praying disciples with a fullness that reached every heart. The Infinite One revealed Himself in power to His church. It was as if for ages this influence had been held in restraint, and now Heaven rejoiced in being able to pour out upon the church the riches of the Spirit's grace. And under the influence of the Spirit, words of penitence and confession mingled with songs of praise for sins forgiven. Words of thanksgiving and of prophecy were heard. All heaven bent low to behold and to adore the wisdom of matchless, incomprehensible love. Lost in wonder, the apostles exclaimed, "Herein is love." They grasped the imparted gift. And what followed? The sword of the Spirit, newly edged with power and bathed in the lightnings of heaven, cut its way through unbelief. Thousands were converted in a day.

"It is expedient for you that I go away," Christ had said to His disciples; "for if I go not away, the Comforter will not come unto you; but if I depart, I will send Him unto you." "When He, the Spirit of truth, is come, He will guide you into all truth: for He shall not speak of Himself; but whatsoever He shall hear, that shall He speak: and He will show you things to come." John 16:7, 13.

Christ's ascension to heaven was the signal that His followers were to receive the promised blessing. For this they were to wait before they entered upon their work. When Christ passed within the heavenly gates, He was enthroned amidst the adoration of the angels. As soon as this ceremony was completed, the Holy Spirit descended upon the disciples in rich currents, and Christ was indeed glorified, even **[page 39]** with the glory which He had with the Father from all eternity. The Pentecostal outpouring was Heaven's communication that the Redeemer's inauguration was accomplished. According to His promise He had sent the Holy Spirit from heaven to His followers as a token that He had, as priest and king, received all authority in heaven and on earth, and was the Anointed One over His people.

"And there appeared unto them cloven tongues like as of fire, and it sat upon each of them. And they were all filled with the Holy Ghost, and began to speak with other tongues, as the Spirit gave them utterance." The Holy Spirit, assuming the form of tongues of fire, rested upon those assembled. This was an emblem of the gift then bestowed on the disciples, which enabled them to speak with fluency languages with which they had heretofore been unacquainted. The appearance of fire signified the fervent zeal with which the apostles would labor and the power that would attend their work.

"There were dwelling at Jerusalem Jews, devout men, out of every nation under heaven."

> *This diversity of languages would have been a great hindrance to the proclamation of the gospel; God therefore in a miraculous manner supplied the deficiency of the apostles.*

During the dispersion the Jews had been scattered to almost every part of the inhabited world, and in their exile they had learned to speak various languages. Many of these Jews were on this occasion in Jerusalem, attending the religious festivals then in progress. Every known tongue was represented by those assembled. This diversity of languages would have been a great hindrance to the proclamation of the gospel; God therefore in a miraculous manner supplied the deficiency of the apostles. The Holy Spirit did for them that which **[page 40]** they could not have accomplished for themselves in a lifetime. They could now proclaim the truths of the gospel abroad, speaking with accuracy the languages of those for whom they were laboring. This miraculous gift was a strong evidence to the world that their commission bore the signet of Heaven. From this time forth the language of the disciples was pure, simple, and accurate, whether they spoke in their native tongue or in a foreign language.

> From this time forth the language of the disciples was pure, simple, and accurate, whether they spoke in their native tongue or in a foreign language.

"Now when this was noised abroad, the multitude came together, and were confounded, because that every man heard them speak in his own language. And they were all amazed and marveled, saying one to another, Behold, are not all these which speak Galileans? and how hear we every man in our own tongue, wherein we were born?"

The priests and rulers were greatly enraged at this wonderful manifestation, but they dared not give way to their malice, for fear of exposing themselves to the violence of the people. They had put the Nazarene to death; but here were His servants, unlettered men of Galilee, telling in all the languages then spoken, the story of His life and ministry. The priests, determined to account for the miraculous power of the disciples in some natural way, declared that they were drunken from partaking largely of the new wine prepared for the feast. Some of the most ignorant of the people present seized upon this suggestion as the truth, but the more intelligent knew it to be false; and those who understood the different languages testified to the accuracy with which these languages were used by the disciples. **[page 41]**

In answer to the accusation of the priests Peter showed that this demonstration was in direct fulfillment of the prophecy of Joel, wherein he foretold that such power would come upon men to fit them for a special work. "Ye men of Judea, and all ye that dwell at Jerusalem," he said, "be this known unto you, and hearken to my words: for these are not drunken, as ye suppose, seeing it is but the third hour of the day. But this is that which was spoken by the prophet Joel: And it shall come to pass in the last days, saith God, I will pour out of My Spirit upon all flesh: and your sons and your daughters shall prophesy, and your young men shall see visions, and your old men shall dream dreams: and on My servants and on My handmaidens I will pour out in those days of My Spirit; and they shall prophesy."

With clearness and power Peter bore witness of the death and resurrection of Christ: "Ye men of Israel, hear these words: Jesus of Nazareth, a man approved of God among you by miracles and wonders and signs, which God did by Him in the midst of you, as ye yourselves also know: Him . . . ye have taken, and by wicked hands have crucified and slain: whom God hath raised up, having loosed the pains of death: because it was not possible that He should be holden of it."

# Day 4: Honest Confession

Peter did not refer to the teachings of Christ to prove his position, because he knew that the prejudice of his hearers was so great that his words on this subject would be of no effect. Instead, he spoke to them of David, who was regarded by the Jews as one of the patriarchs of their nation. "David speaketh concerning Him," he declared: "I foresaw the [page 42] Lord always before My face, for He is on My right hand, that I should not be moved: therefore did My heart rejoice, and My tongue was glad; moreover also My flesh shall rest in hope: because Thou wilt not leave My soul in hell, neither wilt Thou suffer Thine Holy One to see corruption. . . .

"Men and brethren, let me freely speak unto you of the patriarch David, that he is both dead and buried, and his sepulcher is with us unto this day." "He . . . spake of the resurrection of Christ, that His soul was not left in hell, neither His flesh did see corruption. This Jesus hath God raised up, whereof we all are witnesses."

The scene is one full of interest. Behold the people coming from all directions to hear the disciples witness to the truth as it is in Jesus. They press in, crowding the temple. Priests and rulers are there, the dark scowl of malignity still on their faces, their hearts still filled with abiding hatred against Christ, their hands uncleansed from the blood shed when they crucified the world's Redeemer. They had thought to find the apostles cowed with fear under the strong hand of oppression and murder, but they find them lifted above all fear and filled with the Spirit, proclaiming with power the divinity of Jesus of Nazareth. They hear them declaring with boldness that the One so recently humiliated, derided, smitten by cruel hands, and crucified, is the Prince of life, now exalted to the right hand of God.

*They comprehended with perfect clearness the object of Christ's mission and the nature of His kingdom. They could speak with power of the Saviour; and as they unfolded to their hearers the plan of salvation, many were convicted and convinced.*

Some of those who listened to the apostles had taken an active part in the condemnation and death of Christ. Their voices had mingled with the rabble in calling for His cruci-[page 43]fixion. When Jesus and Barabbas stood before them in the judgment hall and Pilate asked, "Whom will ye that I release unto you?" they had shouted, "Not this Man, but Barabbas!" Matthew 27:17; John 18:40. When Pilate delivered Christ to them, saying, "Take ye Him, and crucify Him: for I find no fault in Him;" "I am innocent of the blood of this just Person," they had cried, "His blood be on us, and on our children." John 19:6; Matthew 27:24, 25.

Now they heard the disciples declaring that it was the Son of God who had been crucified. Priests and rulers trembled. Conviction and anguish seized the people. "They were pricked in their heart, and said unto Peter and to the rest of the apostles, Men and brethren, what shall we do?" Among those who listened to the disciples were devout Jews, who were sincere in their belief. The power that accompanied the words of the speaker convinced them that Jesus was indeed the Messiah.

"Then Peter said unto them, Repent, and be baptized every one of you in the name of Jesus Christ for the remission of sins, and ye shall receive the gift of the Holy Ghost. For the promise is unto you, and to your children, and to all that are afar off, even as many as the Lord our God shall call."

Peter urged home upon the convicted people the fact that they had rejected Christ because they had been deceived by priests and rulers; and that if they continued to look to these men for counsel, and waited for them to acknowledge Christ before they dared to do so, they would never accept Him. These powerful men, though making a profession **[page 44]** of godliness, were ambitious for earthly riches and glory. They were not willing to come to Christ to receive light.

Under the influence of this heavenly illumination the scriptures that Christ had explained to the disciples stood out before them with the luster of perfect truth. The veil that had prevented them from seeing to the end of that which had been abolished, was now removed, and they comprehended with perfect clearness the object of Christ's mission and the nature of His kingdom. They could speak with power of the Saviour; and as they unfolded to their hearers the plan of salvation, many were convicted and convinced. The traditions and superstitions inculcated by the priests were swept away from their minds, and the teachings of the Saviour were accepted.

*The conversions that took place on the Day of Pentecost were the result of this sowing, the harvest of Christ's work, revealing the power of His teaching.*

"Then they that gladly received his word were baptized: and the same day there were added unto them about three thousand souls."

The Jewish leaders had supposed that the work of Christ would end with His death; but, instead of this, they witnessed the marvelous scenes of the Day of Pentecost. They heard the disciples, endowed with a power and energy hitherto unknown, preaching Christ, their words confirmed by signs and wonders. In Jerusalem, the stronghold of Judaism, thousands openly declared their faith in Jesus of Nazareth as the Messiah.

The disciples were astonished and overjoyed at the greatness of the harvest of souls. They did not regard this wonderful ingathering as the result of their own efforts; they realized that they were entering into other men's labors. **[page 45]** Ever since the fall of Adam, Christ had been committing to chosen servants the seed of His word, to be sown in human hearts. During His life on this earth He had sown the seed of truth and had watered it with His blood. The conversions that took place on the Day of Pentecost were the result of this sowing, the harvest of Christ's work, revealing the power of His teaching.

The arguments of the apostles alone, though clear and convincing, would not have removed the prejudice that had withstood so much evidence. But the Holy Spirit sent the arguments home to hearts with divine power. The words of the apostles were as sharp arrows of the Almighty, convicting men of their terrible guilt in rejecting and crucifying the Lord of glory.

# Section 3: Applying Divine Counsel

## Expecting the Miraculous

The miraculous results the disciples experienced on the Day of Pentecost were the result of a series of at least three convergent factors. These factors came together at the right time. (1) Our ascended Lord was welcomed home by His Father, (2) the disciples prepared their hearts, and (3) the seed of the gospel sown by Jesus blossomed into a glorious harvest. When the time is right and hearts are prepared through earnest prayer, a deeper faith experience, and honest confession, then at Heaven's command, the Holy Spirit is poured out.

1. What was the "signal" to Christ's followers that all Heaven was now ready to pour out the Holy Spirit? (See *The Acts of the Apostles,* page 38, last paragraph, and page 39, paragraph 1.)

   _____

   _____

   _____

2. What is the genuine "gift of tongues"? What is the purpose of the gift of tongues? (See Acts 2:5, 6 and *The Acts of the Apostles,* page 39, paragraph 2.)

   _____

   _____

   _____

3. What does the outpouring of the "gift of tongues" at Pentecost tell you about God? What lessons does it have for the church in the twenty-first century? (See Act 2:7, 8; 1 Corinthians 12:1–13; *The Acts of the Apostles,* page 39, last paragraph, and page 40, paragraph 1.)

   _____

   _____

   _____

4. What Old Testament prophecy did Peter quote to prove that the outpouring of the Holy Spirit on the Day of Pentecost was genuine? (See Joel 2:28–32 and *The Acts of the Apostles,* page 41.)

   _____

   _____

   _____

The Old Testament prophet Joel predicted that the Holy Spirit would be poured out on:

A. "Your sons and your daughters"—The Holy Spirit is given regardless of gender.
B. "Your old men . . . your young men"—The Holy Spirit is given regardless of age.
C. "Menservants and . . . maidservants"—The Holy Spirit is given regardless of social or economic status.

The Holy Spirit will be poured out on "all flesh." The gift of the Holy Spirit is not reserved for some "elite" super-spiritual few. It is given by God to all who meet the conditions. It is for all who come seeking Him with humble hearts, confessing their sin, and believing His promises. (See *The Acts of the Apostles,* p. 50.)

What impact did the disciples' preaching have upon the Jewish leaders, the crowds at Jerusalem, and the disciples themselves? (See *The Acts of the Apostles,* pages 44, 45.)

5. The impact upon the Jewish leaders (See *The Acts of the Apostles,* page 44, paragraph 3.)

_____

_____

_____

6. The impact upon the disciples (See *The Acts of the Apostles,* page 44, paragraph 4, and page 45, paragraph 1.)

_____

_____

_____

7. The impact upon the crowds (See Acts 2:41, 42.)

_____

_____

_____

When the Holy Spirit is poured out in His fullness, the impact is dramatic. As we open our hearts to the outpouring of the Holy Spirit, we, too, will have a significant impact on those around us. God will use us in powerful ways to reach others for His kingdom. We can expect God to open unusual doors of opportunity to share His Word with our family, friends, neighbors, and work associates. As we intercede for the people in our sphere of influence, God will do "exceedingly, abundantly above all that we ask or think" (Ephesians 3:20). William Carey, who was called the father of modern missions, admonished his followers to "Expect great things from God, attempt great things for God." Reach out by faith to receive all that God has for you. You can expect Him to work in ways that will amaze you.

# Day 5

# Loving Unity

Years ago, early in my ministry, I was invited to conduct a Week of Spiritual Emphasis at a Christian elementary school. As the week progressed, it became obvious to me that two of the teachers were having a serious conflict. Their negative attitudes toward one another regularly boiled over in staff meetings. If one suggested an idea, the other opposed it. When both of them were present in a meeting, tension filled the air. It was apparent that they did not like one another at all.

Toward the end of the week, I preached on Christ's great intercessory prayer in John 17. Jesus was about ready to leave His disciples. Soon He would be betrayed and crucified. He would rise from the grave and ascend to His Father. His earnest prayer reflects what was on His heart. It reveals what was on His mind just before His death on the cross. The Savior was concerned about the unity of the church. He prayed, "That they all may be one, as You, Father, are in Me, and I in You; that they also may be one in Us, that the world may believe that You sent me" (John 17:21). Christ longed that the dissension, jealousy, striving for supremacy, and conflict between His disciples cease. He prayed that their unity in spite of all of their differences would reveal to the world the power of His love.

> Christ longed that the dissension, jealousy, striving for supremacy, and conflict between His disciples cease.

As I shared the longing of Jesus' heart with these students and teachers, something remarkable happened. The last night of our Week of Spiritual Emphasis, we scheduled a foot-washing and Communion service. The Holy Spirit broke through. God moved powerfully. The two teachers who experienced such division knelt at each other's feet. The Spirit of God broke down the barriers. They embraced, confessed their negative attitudes, and prayed together.

## The desire for supremacy banished

The disciples before Pentecost also had attitudes of selfish ambition. Prompted by her sons' desire for supremacy, the mother of James and John appealed to Jesus that each of them have a prominent place in what they believed was His soon-coming earthly kingdom.

> The disciples did not ask for a blessing for themselves. They were weighted with the burden of souls.

"She said to Him, 'Grant that these two sons of mine may sit, one on Your right hand and the other on the left, in Your kingdom' " (Matthew 20:21). This request, of course, led to jealousy and disunity among the other disciples. They simply were not ready for the outpouring of the Holy Spirit in Pentecostal power. This is one of the main reasons why Jesus urged them to spend ten days praying together in the Upper Room. For unity must precede the outpouring of the Holy Spirit.

As they sought God in prayer, the Holy Spirit knit their hearts together in Christian love. The Acts account records, "These all continued with one accord in prayer and supplication, with the women and Mary the mother of Jesus, and with His brothers" (Acts 1:14). The record continues in Acts 2:1: "Now when the Day of Pentecost had fully come, they were all with one accord in one place." Commenting on the disciples' experience in the Upper Room, Ellen White states,

> Notice that it was after the disciples had come into perfect unity, when they were no longer striving for the highest place, that the Spirit was poured out. They were of one accord. All differences had been put away. And the testimony borne of them after the Spirit had been given is the same. Mark the word: "The multitude of them that believed were of one heart and of one soul." Acts 4:32. The Spirit of Him who died that sinners might live animated the entire congregation of believers.
>
> The disciples did not ask for a blessing for themselves. They were weighted with the burden of souls. The gospel was to be carried to the ends of the earth, and they claimed the endowment of power that Christ had promised. Then it was that the Holy Spirit was poured out, and thousands were converted in a day (*Testimonies for the Church,* vol. 8, pp. 20, 21).

During those ten days in the Upper Room, the disciples confessed their petty differences toward one another. They repented of their jealousy and pride. Their hearts were filled with love for the Christ who gave His life for them and who now was at the Father's right hand interceding in their behalf. Their selfish ambitions were swallowed up in their love for Christ.

# Day 5: Loving Unity

The disciples discovered that "unity with Christ establishes a bond of unity with one another. This unity is the most convincing proof to the world of the majesty and virtue of Christ, and of His power to take away sin" (Ellen G. White Comments, *The Seventh-day Adventist Bible Commentary*, vol. 5, p. 1148).

> Every believer has gifts that are valuable for building up the body of Christ.

## The basis of biblical unity

This leads us to some practical questions regarding unity. Does unity mean there are no differences of opinion? How could the disciples with such different dispositions and personalities ever enter into complete unity? Does unity imply a merging of our distinct personalities into some divine oneness of thought? Here are five fundamental principles that form the foundation of the unity about which Christ spoke:

1. We have a common Creator. God has made of one blood all nations. We are one by virtue of the fact that we have a common Father. He created us (Acts 17:26).
2. We have a common Redeemer. We are one by virtue of the fact that He redeemed us (Ephesians 2:14–22).
3. We have a common heritage. We are part of the body of Christ, gifted by God for service. Some have greater gifts than others, but every believer has gifts that are valuable for building up the body of Christ (1 Corinthians 12:4–11, 18–21).
4. We have a common message. The disciples were united through a common present-truth message that distinguished them from the world (Ephesians 4:12, 13; Revelation 14:6–12).
5. We have a common mission. The disciples were united through Christ's Great Commission to reach the world with the gospel. Their own selfish ambitions, pride, and desire for supremacy were consumed on the altar of commitment to take the gospel to the world (Matthew 28:18–20).

As the disciples spent time seeking God in prayer, the Holy Spirit impressed their minds that they had a common Creator, Redeemer, heritage, message, and mission. The things that united them were far greater than anything that divided them. And they discovered that the things that divided them were not very important at all. Ellen White describes their unity in these words:

> As the disciples spent time seeking God in prayer, the Holy Spirit impressed their minds that they had a common Creator, Redeemer, heritage, message, and mission.

In these first disciples was presented marked diversity. They were to be the world's teachers, and they represented widely varied types of character. In order successfully to carry forward the work to which they had been called, these men, differing in natural characteristics and in habits of life, needed to come into unity of feeling, thought, and action. This unity it was Christ's object to secure. To this end He sought to bring them into unity with Himself. The burden of His labor for them is expressed in His prayer to His Father, "That they all may be one; as Thou, Father, art in Me, and I in Thee, that they also may be one in Us;" "that the world may know that Thou has sent Me, and hast loved them, as Thou hast loved Me." John 17:21, 23. His constant prayer for them was that they might be sanctified through the truth; and He prayed with assurance, knowing that an Almighty decree had been given before the world was made. He knew that the gospel of the kingdom would be preached to all nations for a witness; He knew that truth armed with the omnipotence of the Holy Spirit, would conquer in the battle with evil, and that the bloodstained banner would one day wave triumphantly over His followers (*The Acts of the Apostles,* pp. 20, 21).

> *In spite of their personality differences, through Christ these early Christians had a love for one another that was evident to those observing them.*

The phrase "unity of feeling, thought, and action" is a fascinating expression. What precisely is unity of feeling, unity of thought, and unity of action? Unity of feeling refers to a genuine love and respect for one another. In spite of their personality differences, through Christ these early Christians had a love for one another that was evident to those observing them. The apostle John counseled believers with these words, "Beloved, let us love one another, for love is of God; and everyone who loves is born of God" (1 John 4:7). Unity of thought refers to a common core belief system. The disciples were unified in Christ and His teachings. Their confidence in His teachings unified them. Their understanding of the truth He taught brought them together. Their acceptance of the doctrines He espoused gave them a common focus. Unity of action refers to their understanding and acceptance of their mission. The disciples were focused on the completion of the task the Master had given them. They were passionate about proclaiming the message of His love to the world. They were consumed with sharing the gospel everywhere possible. They would not allow their different personality traits, ways of viewing varied issues, or personal preferences to stand in the way of accomplishing Christ's mission. This leads us to some critically important questions for our lives today. On your knees, why not prayerfully consider the five questions below? Use them as subject matter for prayer. If you are studying this manual in a small-group setting, you may want to discuss the questions before praying about them.

1. Are there times when my personal opinions create conflict in my home or church? What might I do to reduce that conflict?
2. If I have feelings of hostility toward another member of the church, what practical steps can I take to reduce the conflict?
3. If I have been wronged unnecessarily and am struggling to relate to the one who hurt me, how can I take the initiative to bridge the chasm in the relationship?
4. If I am a local church leader, what can I do to foster unity?
5. How does personal involvement in mission foster church unity? Am I involved in some aspect of soul winning? If not, why not ask Jesus to guide me into what He wants me to do?

# Section 2: Reflecting on Divine Counsel

Thoughtfully read the following excerpt from *The Acts of the Apostles,* pages 45–50.

Ever since the fall of Adam, Christ had been committing to chosen servants the seed of His word, to be sown in human hearts. During His life on this earth He had sown the seed of truth and had watered it with His blood. The conversions that took place on the Day of Pentecost were the result of this sowing, the harvest of Christ's work, revealing the power of His teaching.

The arguments of the apostles alone, though clear and convincing, would not have removed the prejudice that had withstood so much evidence. But the Holy Spirit sent the arguments home to hearts with divine power. The words of the apostles were as sharp arrows of the Almighty, convicting men of their terrible guilt in rejecting and crucifying the Lord of glory.

Under the training of Christ the disciples had been led to feel their need of the Spirit. Under the Spirit's teaching they received the final qualification, and went forth to their lifework. No longer were they ignorant and uncultured. No longer were they a collection of independent units or discordant, conflicting elements. No longer were their hopes set on worldly greatness. They were of "one accord," "of one heart and of one soul." Acts 2:46; 4:32. Christ filled their thoughts; the advancement of His kingdom was their aim. In mind and character they had become like their Master, and men "took knowledge of them, that they had been with Jesus." Acts 4:13.

> *P*entecost brought them the heavenly illumination. The truths they could not understand while Christ was with them were now unfolded.

Pentecost brought them the heavenly illumination. The truths they could not understand while Christ was with them were now unfolded. With a faith and assurance that **[page 46]** they had never before known, they accepted the teachings of the Sacred Word. No longer was it a matter of faith with them that Christ was the Son of God. They knew that, although clothed with humanity, He was indeed the Messiah, and they told their experience to the world with a confidence which carried with it the conviction that God was with them.

They could speak the name of Jesus with assurance; for was He not their Friend and Elder Brother? Brought into close communion with Christ, they sat with Him in heavenly places. With what burning language they clothed their ideas as they bore witness for Him! Their hearts were surcharged with a benevolence so full, so deep, so far-reaching, that it impelled them to go to the ends of the earth, testifying to the power of Christ. They were filled with an intense longing to carry forward the work He had begun. They realized the greatness of their debt to heaven and the responsibility of their work. Strengthened by the endowment of the Holy Spirit, they went forth filled with zeal to extend the triumphs of the cross. The Spirit animated them and spoke through them. The peace of Christ shone from their faces. They had consecrated their lives to Him for service, and their very features bore evidence to the surrender they had made. **[page 47]**

When Christ gave His disciples the promise of the Spirit, He was nearing the close of His earthly ministry. He was standing in the shadow of the cross, with a full realization of the load of guilt that was to rest upon Him as the Sin Bearer. Before offering Himself as the sacrificial victim, He instructed His disciples regarding a most essential and complete gift which He was to bestow upon His followers—the gift that would bring within their reach the boundless resources of His grace. "I will pray the Father," He said, "and He shall give you another Comforter, that He may abide with you forever; even the Spirit of truth; whom the world cannot receive, because it seeth Him not, neither knoweth Him: but ye know Him; for He dwelleth with you, and shall be in you." John 14:16, 17. The Saviour was pointing forward to the time when the Holy Spirit should come to do a mighty work as His representative. The evil that had been accumulating for centuries [page 48] was to be resisted by the divine power of the Holy Spirit.

> *The church beheld converts flocking to her from all directions.*

What was the result of the outpouring of the Spirit on the Day of Pentecost? The glad tidings of a risen Saviour were carried to the uttermost parts of the inhabited world. As the disciples proclaimed the message of redeeming grace, hearts yielded to the power of this message. The church beheld converts flocking to her from all directions. Backsliders were reconverted. Sinners united with believers in seeking the pearl of great price. Some who had been the bitterest opponents of the gospel became its champions. The prophecy was fulfilled, "He that is feeble . . . shall be as David; and the house of David . . . as the angel of the Lord." Zechariah 12:8. Every Christian saw in his brother a revelation of divine love and benevolence. One interest prevailed; one subject of emulation swallowed up all others. The ambition of the believers was to reveal the likeness of Christ's character and to labor for the enlargement of His kingdom.

"With great power gave the apostles witness of the resurrection of the Lord Jesus: and great grace was upon them all." Acts 4:33. Under their labors were added to the church chosen men, who, receiving the word of truth, consecrated their lives to the work of giving to others the hope that filled their hearts with peace and joy. They could not be restrained or intimidated by threatenings. The Lord spoke through them, and as they went from place to place, the poor had the gospel preached to them, and miracles of divine grace were wrought. [page 49] So mightily can God work when men give themselves up to the control of His Spirit.

> *The promise of the Holy Spirit is not limited to any age or to any race.*

The promise of the Holy Spirit is not limited to any age or to any race. Christ declared that the divine influence of His Spirit was to be with His followers unto the end. From the Day of Pentecost to the present time, the Comforter has been sent to all who have yielded themselves fully to the Lord and to His service. To all who have accepted Christ as a personal Saviour, the Holy Spirit has come as a counselor, sanctifier, guide, and witness. The more closely believers have walked with God, the more clearly and powerfully have they testified of their Redeemer's love and of His saving grace. The men and women who through the long centuries of persecution and trial enjoyed a large measure of the presence of the Spirit in their lives, have stood as signs and wonders in the world. Before angels and men they have revealed the transforming power of redeeming love.

Those who at Pentecost were endued with power from on high, were not thereby freed from further temptation and trial. As they witnessed for truth and righteousness they were repeatedly assailed by the enemy of all truth, who sought to rob them of their Christian experience. They were compelled to strive with all their God-given powers to reach the measure of the stature of men and women in Christ Jesus. Daily they prayed for fresh supplies of grace, that they might reach higher and still higher toward perfection. Under the Holy Spirit's working even the weakest, **[page 50]** by exercising faith in God, learned to improve their entrusted powers and to become sanctified, refined, and ennobled. As in humility they submitted to the molding influence of the Holy Spirit, they received of the fullness of the Godhead and were fashioned in the likeness of the divine.

> *Those who at Pentecost were endued with power from on high, were not thereby freed from further temptation and trial.*

## Section 3: Applying Divine Counsel
### Uniting in Mission

During the ten days in the Upper Room, the disciples entered into the unity that Jesus prayed for in His great intercessory prayer in John 17. Once they became of "one accord," they were now ready to receive the promised Holy Spirit. The seeds Jesus had sown during His earthly ministry would spring up to bear an abundant harvest under the showers of the Spirit's blessing at Pentecost.

1. How did Jesus' earthly ministry influence what happened on the Day of Pentecost? (See *The Acts of the Apostles,* page 45, paragraph 1.)

   _____

   _____

   _____

The Savior did not see the full extent of His work while He was on earth. In fact, when Jesus died, it appeared His work was a failure. "As the world's redeemer, Christ was constantly confronted with apparent failure. He, the messenger of mercy to our world, seemed to do little of the work He longed to do in uplifting and saving" (*The Desire of Ages,* p. 678).

### The full impact of Jesus' work was only seen after His ascension at Pentecost.

In describing the growth of the New Testament church, the apostle Paul reminded the Corinthian believers, "I planted, Apollos watered, but God gave the increase. So neither he who plants is anything, nor he who waters, but God who gives the increase. Now he who plants and he who waters are one, and each one will receive his own reward according to his own labor. For we are God's fellow workers" (1 Corinthians 3:6–9).

All success in God's work comes as we recognize that our role is to be faithful to God. We may never see the full results of our work, but if we do our part, God will use others who do their part to reach honest-hearted souls with the gospel.

2. In Acts 1:14; 2:1; and 2:46, Luke records that the disciples were of "one accord." What does this mean? What is the significance of being in "one accord" to the church today? (See *The Acts of the Apostles,* page 45, paragraph 2.)

   A. The meaning of "one accord" is

   _____

   _____

   _____

# Day 5: Loving Unity

B. The significance of being in "one accord" for the church today is

_____

_____

_____

3. How did the outpouring of the Holy Spirit on the Day of Pentecost make a difference in the witness of the disciples? (See Acts 4:20, 31, 33; 5:42; and *The Acts of the Apostles,* page 45, last paragraph, and page 46.)

_____

_____

_____

4. What was the result of the outpouring of the Holy Spirit on the Day of Pentecost? (See Acts 2:41; 4:4; 5:15; 6:7; 9:31; and *The Acts of the Apostles,* page 48, paragraph 1.)

_____

_____

_____

5. Was Christ's promise of the Holy Spirit limited to the disciples at Pentecost? (See Luke 11:13 and *The Acts of the Apostles,* page 49.)

_____

_____

_____

The promise of the Holy Spirit is for each generation. God wants to do more in us and through us than we can possibly imagine. At the time of the end, the Pentecost will be repeated in greater measure. The power of God will be poured out in its fullness to finish His work on earth. As God's people enter into unity based on a common message, movement, and mission, God will pour out His Spirit in abundant measure for the finishing of His work on earth.

# Day 6
## Self-Examination

At Pentecost the time was right, and the disciples were ready. Jesus had ascended to His Father. His sacrifice was accepted at God's throne. Then He received the promised Holy Spirit from His Father for His earthly disciples to accomplish their God-given mission. They heeded our Lord's counsel. They sought Him in prayer. They experienced heartfelt repentance and confessed the specific sins the Holy Spirit brought to their minds. During those ten days in the Upper Room, they drew close in Christian unity. Luke records that "the multitude of those who believed were of one heart and one soul" (Acts 4:32). Petty jealousies were laid aside. Strife and alienation were banished. Personal conflicts were resolved. Barriers were broken down.

Although the Bible does not give us a detailed account of what actually happened in the Upper Room, it provides us with enough information to develop an outline of what actually took place. The modern-day gift of prophecy helps us to fill in the details of this outline and illuminates the biblical record. One of the vitally important details that Ellen White points out is that "these days of preparation were days of deep heart searching. The disciples felt their spiritual need and cried to the Lord for the holy unction that was to fit them for the work of soul saving" (*The Acts of the Apostles,* p. 37). The ten days in the Upper Room were days of deep heart searching. They were days of reflection and self-examination. "After Christ's ascension, the disciples were gathered together in one place to make humble supplication to God. And after ten days of heart searching and self-examination, the way was prepared for the Holy Spirit to enter the cleansed, consecrated soul temples" (*Evangelism,* p. 698). The disciples wanted to be sure that there were no attitudes or habits in their lives that would hinder the outpouring of the Holy Spirit. They spent time examining their hearts. They wanted to be sure that their motives were pure.

## Searching our hearts

Throughout the Bible, God admonishes us to spend time examining our hearts. The apostle Paul urges us to look "diligently lest anyone fall short of the grace of God; lest any root of bitterness springing up cause trouble, and by this many become defiled" (Hebrews 12:15). Roots produce shoots and shoots produce fruits. If there is a root of bitterness in your heart, it will produce the shoots of anger, criticism, or gossip, and will result in the tragic fruit of a broken relationship. All sinful roots will eventually produce their ugly fruits.

> If there is a root of bitterness in your heart, it will produce the shoots of anger, criticism, or gossip, and will result in the tragic fruit of a broken relationship.

Many years ago my wife and I visited Fort Ticonderoga in New Hampshire. This Revolutionary War fort was a strategic military outpost from 1775 to 1779. Knowing that some tourists regularly found arrowheads near the walls of the fort, I asked our guide where to look. He smiled and calmly replied, "Right by the main gate." I was somewhat startled. How could there be any arrowheads there when thousands of people entered the main gate each year? Why hadn't they found them before? The guide explained that the best time to find arrowheads was when the spring thaw brought them to the surface after the long New England winter. I have thought of our guide's explanation numerous times. The arrowheads were a few inches beneath the surface, but it took the warmth of the spring thaw to bring them up. Do arrowheads of sin lurk just below the surface in your heart that only the gentle rains of the Holy Spirit can bring to the surface? King David prayed, "Examine me, O LORD, and prove me; try my mind and my heart. For Your lovingkindness is before my eyes, and I have walked in Your truth" (Psalm 26:2, 3).

When we see God's loving-kindness and observe the righteousness of His character, we recognize our weakness, shortcomings, and sins. In the blazing light of His unconditional love and perfection, our hearts are humbled. We are led to deep confession and repentance. We cry out to Him for the salvation and righteousness that only He can provide. When we are overwhelmed with His holiness, with the prophet Isaiah, we cry out, "Woe is me, for I am undone!" (Isaiah 6:5). Self-examination may not always be the most pleasant experience, but it is absolutely necessary. In self-examination we ask God, "Is there anything in my life that is not in harmony with Your will?" We pray, "Lord, reveal those attitudes deep within my soul that are not like Jesus."

> Self-examination may not always be the most pleasant experience, but it is absolutely necessary.

## A practical example of self-examination

Ellen White gives us a practical example of the need for self-examination. "In the family if one member is lost to God every means should be used for his recovery. On the part of all the others let there be diligent, careful self-examination. Let the life-practice be investigated. See if there is

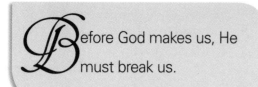

Before God makes us, He must break us.

not some mistake, some error in management, by which that soul is confirmed in impenitence" (*Christ's Object Lessons,* p. 194). Self-examination may be painful at times. The Holy Spirit may reveal things about ourselves that we have not known before. Traits that we have not been conscious of may be brought to the surface. The Lord does not reveal these unchristlike characteristics to discourage us. He reveals them so we can confess and surrender them to Him to receive His pardon and cleansing. He wants to heal the broken relationships in our past. He longs to transform our lives and give us a future filled with hope. He longs to replace our anxiety over the mistakes of the past with a confidence in His guidance in the present. If we have made mistakes in raising our children, let's confess them to God and ask Him to empower us to make the necessary changes. If necessary, let's share with our teenagers the mistakes we have made and ask their forgiveness.

The purpose of self-examination is to discover those areas of our lives that have been hidden from our eyes. All of us have blind spots about recognizing defects in our characters. At times the Holy Spirit leads us to take a spiritual inventory to determine just where those blind spots are. The psalmist prayed, "Search me, O God, and know my heart; try me, and know my anxieties; and see if there is any wicked way in me, and lead me in the way everlasting" (Psalm 139:23, 24). God's goal in this process is to lead us closer to Him. He does not want us to wallow in guilt or be filled with remorse over our past lives. His goal is to lead us "in the way everlasting." Although it is healthy to take a candid look at our own spiritual lives, it is unhealthy to dwell on the faults of our past lives. Dwelling on our faults and focusing too long on our mistakes only discourages us.

Our Lord is bigger than our mistakes and greater than our failures. We certainly need to honestly know our condition—but it is much more important to know His grace. Understanding our weakness prepares us to receive His strength. Understanding our sinfulness prepares us to receive His righteousness. Understanding our ignorance prepares us to receive His wisdom. The Holy Spirit may lead us to lament over our fallen natures, but He does not leave us there. The purpose of the Holy Spirit's conviction is to lead us to Jesus. As we recognize our sins and mistakes through a process of self-examination, we can thank God that the Holy Spirit is leading us closer to Jesus. The convicting power of the Holy Spirit is preparing us to receive the fullness of the Spirit in latter-rain power. Before God makes us, He must break us. Before He fills us, He must empty us. Before He is enthroned in our hearts, self must be dethroned. What a wonderful Savior is Jesus our Lord. His supreme desire is that we reflect His loving character before a waiting world and watching universe. He wants to prepare us now for the greatest outpouring of the Holy Spirit in history.

Prayerfully reflect on the questions below.

1. Is there anything lurking deep within my soul that would hinder me from receiving the fullness of the Holy Spirit?
2. Am I willing to give God permission to take anything out of my life that is not in harmony with His will?
3. Is there something in my life I have been unwilling to surrender?

## Section 2: Reflecting on Divine Counsel

Prayerfully read the excerpt below from *The Acts of the Apostles,* pages 50–52.

The lapse of time has wrought no change in Christ's parting promise to send the Holy Spirit as His representative. It is not because of any restriction on the part of God that the riches of His grace do not flow earthward to men. If the fulfillment of the promise is not seen as it might be, it is because the promise is not appreciated as it should be. If all were willing, all would be filled with the Spirit. Wherever the need of the Holy Spirit is a matter little thought of, there is seen spiritual drought, spiritual darkness, spiritual declension and death. Whenever minor matters occupy the attention, the divine power which is necessary for the growth and prosperity of the church, and which would bring all other blessings in its train, is lacking, though offered in infinite plenitude.

> The Lord is more willing to give the Holy Spirit to those who serve Him than parents are to give good gifts to their children.

Since this is the means by which we are to receive power, why do we not hunger and thirst for the gift of the Spirit? Why do we not talk of it, pray for it, and preach concerning it? The Lord is more willing to give the Holy Spirit to those who serve Him than parents are to give good gifts to their children. For the daily baptism of the Spirit every worker should offer his petition to God. Companies of Christian workers should gather to ask for special help, for heavenly wisdom, that they may know how to plan and execute wisely. Especially should they pray that God will baptize **[page 51]** His chosen ambassadors in mission fields with a rich measure of His Spirit. The presence of the Spirit with God's workers will give the proclamation of truth a power that not all the honor or glory of the world could give.

With the consecrated worker for God, in whatever place he may be, the Holy Spirit abides. The words spoken to the disciples are spoken also to us. The Comforter is ours as well as theirs. The Spirit furnishes the strength that sustains striving, wrestling souls in every emergency, amidst the hatred of the world, and the realization of their

> With the consecrated worker for God, in whatever place he may be, the Holy Spirit abides.

own failures and mistakes. In sorrow and affliction, when the outlook seems dark and the future perplexing, and we feel helpless and alone—these are the times when, in answer to the prayer of faith, the Holy Spirit brings comfort to the heart.

It is not a conclusive evidence that a man is a Christian because he manifests spiritual ecstasy under extraordinary circumstances. Holiness is not rapture: it is an entire surrender of the will to God; it is living by every word that proceeds from the mouth of God; it is doing the will of our heavenly Father; it is trusting God in trial, in darkness as well as in the light; it is walking by faith and not by sight; it is relying on God with unquestioning confidence, and resting in His love.

It is not essential for us to be able to define just what the Holy Spirit is. Christ tells us that the Spirit is the Comforter, "the Spirit of truth, which proceedeth from the Father." It is plainly declared regarding the Holy Spirit that, in His work of guiding men into all truth, "He shall not speak of Himself." John 15:26; 16:13. **[page 52]**

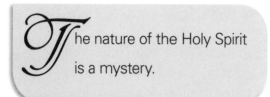
The nature of the Holy Spirit is a mystery.

The nature of the Holy Spirit is a mystery. Men cannot explain it, because the Lord has not revealed it to them. Men having fanciful views may bring together passages of Scripture and put a human construction on them, but the acceptance of these views will not strengthen the church. Regarding such mysteries, which are too deep for human understanding, silence is golden.

The office of the Holy Spirit is distinctly specified in the words of Christ: "When He is come, He will reprove the world of sin, and of righteousness, and of judgment." John 16:8. It is the Holy Spirit that convicts of sin. If the sinner responds to the quickening influence of the Spirit, he will be brought to repentance and aroused to the importance of obeying the divine requirements.

To the repentant sinner, hungering and thirsting for righteousness, the Holy Spirit reveals the Lamb of God that taketh away the sin of the world. "He shall receive of Mine, and shall show it unto you," Christ said. "He shall teach you all things, and bring all things to your remembrance, whatsoever I have said unto you." John 16:14; 14:26.

The Spirit is given as a regenerating agency, to make effectual the salvation wrought by the death of our Redeemer. The Spirit is constantly seeking to draw the attention of men to the great offering that was made on the cross of Calvary, to unfold to the world the love of God, and to open to the convicted soul the precious things of the Scriptures.

# Section 3: Applying Divine Counsel
## Receiving the Spirit

Have you ever wondered why the New Testament church had such spiritual life and at times our churches have so little? Why was the Holy Spirit poured out so abundantly then, and His power seems so feeble now? Why were these early disciples so full of the Holy Spirit, and why are we so devoid of His presence? What is the difference? Possibly it is time for us to do some serious reflection. Maybe the Holy Spirit is leading us to look within our own hearts in self-examination.

1. Has the passing of time made any change in Christ's parting promise to send His Holy Spirit to His church? (See Acts 2:37–39 and *The Acts of the Apostles,* page 50, paragraph 1.)

   _____

   _____

   _____

2. What three reasons does *The Acts of the Apostles,* page 50, paragraph 1, give for the lack of the Holy Spirit's power among us? Complete the sentences below and ask yourself whether any of these characteristics apply to your personal life.

   "The promise is not _____

   _____

   _____." 

   "Wherever the need of the Holy Spirit is a matter _____

   _____

   _____." 

   "Whenever minor matters_____

   _____

   _____." 

## To Think About
- Do I personally fully appreciate the gift of the Holy Spirit that Christ has offered?
- Is receiving the Holy Spirit a priority in my life?
- Do "minor matters" crowd out time for placing priority on the things of eternity?

3. What practical steps has our Lord outlined to prepare us to receive the outpouring of the Holy Spirit? (See *The Acts of the Apostles,* page 50, paragraph 2.)

A. Circle the five verbs in the sentences below.

"Why do we not hunger and thirst for the gift of the Spirit? Why do we not talk of it, pray for it, and preach concerning it?"

Summarize what these five verbs mean in your own spiritual life.

_____

_____

B. Complete the two sentences below.

• "For the daily baptism of the Spirit _____

_____

_____."

• "Companies of Christian workers should _____

_____

_____."

Our Lord invites us to personally open our hearts and petition heaven for the gift of the Holy Spirit as well as to meet with small groups of fellow believers in seeking the reception of the Holy Spirit.

4. What will the Holy Spirit do in the lives of believers who are facing trials, challenges, and difficulties? (See Romans 8:14–17; Ephesians 3:14–21; *The Acts of the Apostles,* page 51, paragraph 1.)

_____

_____

_____

5. What is the greatest evidence that the Holy Spirit has filled our lives? (See *The Acts of the Apostles,* page 81, paragraph 2.)

_____

_____

_____

## Day 6: Self-Examination

The greatest evidence of a Spirit-filled life is a transformed life. It is a mind committed to doing God's will. It is the desire to please God in every aspect of our lives (John 8:29; Hebrews 8:10; 10:7). The greatest evidence of a Spirit-filled life is not the manifestation of supernatural signs. The devil can counterfeit signs and wonders (Revelation 14; 18:20; Matthew 24:24). Will you open your heart to the Holy Spirit's working and ask Him to reveal anything deep within your heart that hinders you from receiving the fullness of the Holy Spirit's power now?

# Day 7

# Sacrificial Humility

The disciples' attitudes before Pentecost were dramatically different from their attitudes after Pentecost. Ten days in the Upper Room made a remarkable difference. Luke's Gospel notes that shortly before Jesus' death, "there was also rivalry among them, as to which of them should be considered the greatest" (Luke 22:24). This certainly does not sound like the description of a group of men who were ordained to model Christ's love in the cities and towns they were called to reach with the message of the Cross. It does not seem like a community of believers who could be trusted with the Holy Spirit's power to turn the world upside down with their preaching. Personal ambitions dominated their thinking. Motivated by self-interest, they were much more interested in what they would receive from following Christ than in giving themselves in selfless service. They were confident that they were ready to rule with Christ in His coming kingdom, and each longed for preeminence.

Peter's confidence overflowed as he brashly uttered that he was willing to go "both to prison and death" for Christ (Luke 22:33). In fact, according to Matthew's Gospel, all of the disciples expressed this same arrogant, self-confident attitude. Peter assured Jesus, " 'Even if I have to die with You, I will not deny You!' And so said all the disciples" (Matthew 26:35). In striving for first place, these disciples failed to understand the essence of the gospel. They seemed deaf to Jesus' words, "Whoever desires to be first among you, let him be your slave—just as the Son of Man did not come to be served, but to serve, and to give His life a ransom for many" (Matthew 20:27, 28).

# Day 7: Sacrificial Humility

## Pentecost makes a difference

Pentecost made all the difference. During the ten days in the Upper Room, the disciples carefully examined their own hearts. They understood their weakness and pleaded for His strength. They realized their frailties and sought for His enduring might. They recognized their selfishness and pleaded for the humble, selfless spirit of Jesus. Describing their experience, Ellen White states,

> As the disciples waited for the fulfillment of the promise, they humbled their hearts in true repentance and confessed their unbelief. As they called to remembrance the words that Christ had spoken to them before His death they understood more fully their meaning. Truths which had passed from their memory were again brought to their minds, and these they repeated to one another. They reproached themselves for their misapprehension of the Saviour. Like a procession, scene after scene of His wonderful life passed before them. As they meditated upon His pure, holy life they felt that no toil would be too hard, no sacrifice too great, if only they could bear witness in their lives to the loveliness of Christ's character. Oh, if they could but have the past three years to live over, they thought, how differently they would act! (*The Acts of the Apostles*, p. 36).

As the disciples prayed together, humbling their hearts before God, the Holy Spirit brought to their minds the lessons of humility, trust, submission, and service that Christ had so longed for them to understand. The disciples felt rebuked by the convicting power of the Holy Spirit. They wished they could live the last three and a half years over again. Have you ever felt that way? Have you ever wished you could go back and correct your past mistakes? The Holy Spirit not only convicts us of sin, He heals our broken hearts. He brings us hope. He assures us that God has a better plan for our lives. He inspires us with promises of a better future.

> The Holy Spirit not only convicts us of sin, He heals our broken hearts.

Take Peter, for example. After Pentecost, he was a totally changed person. Filled with the Holy Spirit, he preached a powerful sermon on the Day of Pentecost, and three thousand people were convicted and were baptized in one day. When the Jewish authorities attempted to silence his witness, he fearlessly exclaimed, "We cannot but speak the things we have seen and heard" (Acts 4:20). The boastful Peter had become confident, not in himself, but in the strength of the Lord. The arrogant Peter had learned the lesson of humble, selfless service. Listen to his own testimony, "All of you be submissive to one another, and be clothed with humility, for 'God resists the proud, but gives grace to the humble.' Therefore humble yourselves under the mighty hand of God, that He may exalt you in due time" (1 Peter 5:5, 6). Humble hearts are hearts that God can fill with His Spirit. They are hearts that are open to receive God's richest blessing.

> Humble hearts are hearts that God can fill with His Spirit. They are hearts that are open to receive God's richest blessing.

### Jesus: Our Example

Consider Jesus. The Savior left the glories of heaven to come to this sinful world. He left the fellowship of the Father, the adoration of the angels, and the worship of heavenly beings. The apostle Paul describes Jesus' experience in these words, "And being found in appearance as a man, He humbled Himself and became obedient to the point of death, even the death of the cross. Therefore God also has highly exalted Him and given Him the name which is above every name" (Philippians 2:8, 9). Jesus not only became a man, He became a servant. He not only became a servant but He became an obedient servant. He not only became an obedient servant but He was obedient unto death. He not only died but He died the most horrible death of all, the death of the cross. Christ's death on the cross qualified Him to become our High Priest in heaven above, seated at the right hand of God. Humble obedience always precedes greatness. God exalts those who bow low in humility.

> Give God permission to take all selfishness and greed out of your heart.

### *Humility* defined

Humility is an attitude of loving service that does not inflate one's own importance. It is constantly concerned about the needs of others. In the humble heart, self is not the center of the universe. Humility leads us to be others centered. Its focus is on giving not on getting. It desires only good for others and does not use them to accomplish its own ends. Humility is one of the characteristics that God values most. Read the three passages below prayerfully and answer the questions that follow.

- "Let nothing be done through selfish ambition or conceit, but in lowliness of mind let each esteem others better than himself. Let each of you look out not only for his own interests, but also for the interests of others" (Philippians 2:3, 4).
- "Therefore, as the elect of God, holy and beloved, put on tender mercies, kindness, humbleness of mind, meekness, longsuffering" (Colossians 3:12).
- "God resists the proud, but gives grace to the humble" (James 4:6).

1. What does it mean for a person to "esteem others better than himself"?
2. What is "lowliness of mind"? How can we "put on" lowliness of mind?
3. Explain why God "resists the proud, but gives grace to the humble."
4. Why is humility so important in receiving the latter rain?

Over the coming days, ask God to give you a humble spirit. Plead with Him to take all pride out of your heart. Seek to have a mind filled with the desire to serve others. Give God permission to take all selfishness and greed out of your heart. The Holy Spirit may reveal pride, selfish ambition, a competitive spirit, or the desire for preeminence. If He does, open your heart to the cleansing power of Jesus and remember that God often humbles us before He fills us—He often brings us low before He exalts us.

# Section 2: Reflecting on Divine Counsel

Thoughtfully read the following excerpt from *The Acts of the Apostles,* pages 53–56.

From the beginning, God has been working by His Holy Spirit through human instrumentalities for the accomplishment of His purpose in behalf of the fallen race. This was manifest in the lives of the patriarchs. To the church in the wilderness also, in the time of Moses, God gave His "good Spirit to instruct them." Nehemiah 9:20. And in the days of the apostles He wrought mightily for His church through the agency of the Holy Spirit. The same power that sustained the patriarchs, that gave Caleb and Joshua faith and courage, and that made the work of the apostolic church effective, has upheld God's faithful children in every succeeding age. It was through the

> *Today God is still using His church to make known His purpose in the earth.*

power of the Holy Spirit that during the Dark Ages the Waldensian Christians helped to prepare the way for the Reformation. It was the same power that made successful the efforts of the noble men and women who pioneered the way for the establishment of modern missions and for the translation of the Bible into the languages and dialects of all nations and peoples.

And today God is still using His church to make known His purpose in the earth. Today the heralds of the cross are going from city to city, and from land to land, preparing **[page 54]** the way for the second advent of Christ. The standard of God's law is being exalted. The Spirit of the Almighty is moving upon men's hearts, and those who respond to its influence become witnesses for God and His truth. In many places consecrated men and women may be seen communicating to others the light that has made plain to them the way of salvation through Christ. And as they continue to let their light shine, as did those who were baptized with the Spirit on the Day of Pentecost, they receive more and still more of the Spirit's power. Thus the earth is to be lightened with the glory of God.

> *The Spirit of the Almighty is moving upon men's hearts, and those who respond to its influence become witnesses for God and His truth.*

On the other hand, there are some who, instead of wisely improving present opportunities, are idly waiting for some special season of spiritual refreshing by which their ability to enlighten others will be greatly increased. They neglect present duties and privileges, and allow their light to burn dim, while they look forward to a time when, without any effort on their part, they will be made the recipients of special blessing, by which they will be transformed and fitted for service.

It is true that in the time of the end, when God's work in the earth is closing, the earnest efforts put forth by consecrated believers under the guidance of the Holy Spirit are to be accompanied by special tokens of divine favor. Under the figure of the early and the latter rain, that falls in Eastern lands at seedtime and harvest, the Hebrew prophets foretold the bestowal of spiritual grace in extraordinary measure upon God's church. The outpouring of the Spirit in the days of the apostles was the beginning of the early, or **[page 55]** former, rain, and glorious was the result. To the end of time the presence of the Spirit is to abide with the true church.

> *Unless the members of God's church today have a living connection with the Source of all spiritual growth, they will not be ready for the time of reaping.*

But near the close of earth's harvest, a special bestowal of spiritual grace is promised to prepare the church for the coming of the Son of man. This outpouring of the Spirit is likened to the falling of the latter rain; and it is for this added power that Christians are to send their petitions to the Lord of the harvest "in the time of the latter rain." In response, "the Lord shall make bright clouds, and give them showers of rain." "He will cause to come down . . . the rain, the former rain, and the latter rain." Zechariah 10:1; Joel 2:23.

But unless the members of God's church today have a living connection with the Source of all spiritual growth, they will not be ready for the time of reaping. Unless they keep their lamps trimmed and burning, they will fail of receiving added grace in times of special need.

Those only who are constantly receiving fresh supplies of grace, will have power proportionate to their daily need and their ability to use that power. Instead of looking forward to some future time when, through a special endowment of spiritual power, they will receive a miraculous fitting up for soul winning, they are yielding themselves daily to God, that He may make them vessels meet for His use. Daily they are improving the opportunities for service that lie within their reach. Daily they are witnessing for the Master wherever they may be, whether in some humble sphere of labor in the home, or in a public field of usefulness. **[page 56]** To the consecrated worker there is wonderful consolation in the knowledge that even Christ during His life on earth sought His Father daily for fresh supplies of needed grace; and from this communion with God He went forth to strengthen and bless others. Behold the Son of God bowed in prayer to His Father! Though He is the Son of God, He strengthens His faith by prayer, and by communion with heaven gathers to Himself power to resist evil and to minister to the needs of men. As the Elder Brother of our race He knows the necessities of those who, compassed with infirmity and living in a world of sin and temptation, still desire to serve Him. He knows that the messengers whom He sees fit to send are weak, erring men; but to all who give themselves wholly to His service He promises divine aid. His own example is an assurance that earnest, persevering supplication to God in faith—faith that leads to entire dependence upon God, and unreserved consecration to His work—will avail to bring to men the Holy Spirit's aid in the battle against sin.

Every worker who follows the example of Christ will be prepared to receive and use the power that God has promised to His church for the ripening of earth's harvest. Morning by morning, as the heralds of the gospel kneel before the Lord and renew their vows of consecration to Him, He will grant them the presence of His Spirit, with its reviving, sanctifying power. As they go forth to the day's duties, they have the assurance that the unseen agency of the Holy Spirit enables them to be "laborers together with God."

# Section 3: Applying Divine Counsel
## Experiencing the Latter Rain

Throughout history God has used people who have humbled their hearts before Him. When God finds people more interested in His glory than in their own, He uses them mightily for the advancement of His kingdom. As the disciples humbled their hearts before His throne, confessing their sins, and committing themselves to do His will, they experienced the outpouring of the Holy Spirit in abundant measure.

1. Is the reception of the Holy Spirit limited to any particular time period? (See Ephesians 5:18; John 16:7; and *The Acts of the Apostles,* pages 53, 54.)

    A. "From the _____, God has been working by His _____ _____ through human instrumentalities for the accomplishment of His purpose in behalf of the fallen race."

    B. "This was manifested in the lives of the _____."

    C. "In the days of the _____ He wrought mightily for His church through the agency of the Holy Spirit."

    D. "The Spirit of the Almighty is moving upon men's hearts, and those who respond to its influence become _____ _____."

2. What promise does our Lord give to those who "continue to let their light shine, as did those who were baptized with the Spirit on the Day of Pentecost"? (See *The Acts of the Apostles,* page 54.)

    _____

    _____

    _____

3. Why will some church members fail to receive the mighty outpouring of the Holy Spirit in latter-rain power? (See Matthew 25:1–10 and *The Acts of the Apostles,* page 54.)

    _____

    _____

    _____

4. How does God describe the extraordinary outpouring of the Holy Spirit just before the second coming of Jesus? (See Zechariah 10:1; Joel 2:23; and *The Acts of the Apostles,* page 54, last paragraph, and page 55, paragraph 1.)

_____

_____

_____

In the agricultural cycle of Israel, the early rain fell in the autumn to promote the growth of the seed when it was first sown. The latter rain fell in the spring at the end of the agricultural cycle to mature the seed and bring it to harvest (Deuteronomy 11:14). The abundance of rain was seen by each Israelite as a sign of God's blessing and favor. God's prophets use the figure of the latter rain to represent the mighty outpouring of the Holy Spirit just before the second coming of Jesus to empower His church to preach His last-day message of truth to the world.

5. Who will receive the latter rain? What prerequisites are necessary to receive this mighty outpouring of the Holy Spirit? (See *The Acts of the Apostles,* pages 55, 56.)

A. "Those only who are _____

_____

_____."

B. "They are yielding themselves _____

_____

_____."

C. When the latter rains falls, "daily they are _____

_____

_____."

D. "Morning by morning, as the heralds of the gospel _____

_____

_____."

What a privilege! What an opportunity! What possibilities! God longs to pour out His Holy Spirit in latter-rain power upon His church today. Will you open your heart right now and ask God if there is anything in your life that would keep you from receiving the fullness of His Spirit today?

# Day 8

# Obedient Surrender

Confronted with the greatest challenge of His life, Jesus quietly slipped away to Gethsemane. He had visited this secluded olive grove overlooking Jerusalem on numerous occasions before. Here He could be alone. He could pour out His soul to His heavenly Father. Away from the jostle and press of the crowds, He could enter into heartfelt communion with God. On this night fraught with eternal consequences, He brought Peter, James, and John with Him. He longed for their companionship and fellowship in prayer at this pivotal moment of earth's history. Jesus was only a short distance from them when He fell on His face and cried out, "O My Father, if it is possible, let this cup pass from Me; nevertheless, not as I will, but as You will" (Matthew 26:39). Recognizing the horrors that lay before Him, Jesus pleaded with the Father to remove the cup of sorrows He was about to drink. If possible He would have avoided Judas's betrayal, Pilate's judgment hall, the Roman lash, the crown of thorns, and the cross. Jesus did not take His coming suffering lightly. In Gethsemane, He fully realized that sin would crush out His life on Calvary. In the face of incredible physical suffering, mental anguish, and emotional trauma, Jesus made a decision to do the Father's will.

Jesus' prayer in Gethsemane summarizes the guiding principle of His life. "Not as I will, but as You will" was Jesus' life commandment. In every decision of life, He was committed to doing the Father's will. This was a lesson His disciples would have to learn later, during the ten days in the Upper Room. In their drowsy stupor, they failed to comprehend the significance of the moment.

The three passages of Scripture below describe Jesus' single-minded focus.

- Speaking prophetically, the psalmist places these words in the mouth of the Savior: "I delight to do Your will, O my God, and Your law is within my heart" (Psalm 40:8).
- "He who sent Me is with Me. The Father has not left Me alone, for I always do those things that please Him" (John 8:29).
- "Then I said, 'Behold I have come—in the volume of the book it is written of Me—to do Your will, O God' " (Hebrews 10:7).

## Jesus' single-minded objective

Jesus' single-minded objective was to do the will of His Father. His entire life gave glory to God. Jesus' obedient surrender to the Father was the channel through which heavenly blessings flowed earthward. Today as well, the power of the Holy Spirit is poured out through surrendered hearts.

> The disciples were passionate about doing Jesus' will.

Do you think that Peter, James, and John heard Jesus' prayer in Gethsemane? Do you think His earnest plea touched their hearts? They must have been amazed at His total commitment to do the Father's will. This absolute, all-out surrender must have had an impact on their lives. Although they did not fully understand His unswerving loyalty before Pentecost, the example of His life deeply impressed them. It was in the Upper Room at Pentecost that they really began to understand what He had been trying to teach them. "Like a procession, scene after scene of His wonderful life passed before them. As they meditated upon His pure, holy life they felt that no toil would be too hard, no sacrifice too great, if only they could bear witness in their lives to the loveliness of Christ's character" (*The Acts of the Apostles,* p. 36). It was in the Upper Room, as the disciples sought God together, that they became totally committed to do the Father's will. "Christ filled their thoughts; the advancement of His kingdom was their aim. In mind and character they had become like their Master, and men 'took knowledge of them, that they had been with Jesus.' Acts 4:13" (*The Acts of the Apostles,* p. 45).

> Faith that leads to submission to Christ's will is the most important thing in the life of each Christian.

## Submission makes a difference

Peter was a different man after Pentecost. He no longer trembled in fear at the accusations of the officers of the temple. When he was confronted by these religious leaders and they demanded that he stop preaching in Jesus' name, the apostle responded, "We ought to obey God rather than men" (Acts 5:29). Under the influence of the Holy Spirit, the example of Jesus made a difference. Like his Master, Peter's single-minded ambition was to do the will of His heavenly Father. This was true of each of these Spirit-filled disciples. They were willing to face persecution, imprisonment, and even death for Christ's sake. Why?

The disciples were passionate about doing Jesus' will. They had laid aside their own personal agendas. Knowing and obeying Christ became the most important thing in their lives. Similarly,

# Day 8: Obedient Surrender

faith that leads to submission to Christ's will is the most important thing in the life of each Christian. Ellen White describes such submission:

The submission which Christ demands, the self-surrender of the will which admits truth in its sanctifying power, which trembles at the word of the Lord, are brought about by the work of the Holy Spirit. There must be a transformation of the entire being, heart, soul, and character. . . . Only at the altar of sacrifice, and from the hand of God, can the selfish, grasping man receive the celestial torch which reveals his own incompetence and leads him to submit to Christ's yoke, to learn His meekness and lowliness.

*They opened their hearts to the fullness of the Holy Spirit's working and totally committed their lives to doing His will.*

As learners we need to meet with God at the appointed place. Then Christ puts us under the guidance of the Spirit, who leads us into all truth, placing our self-importance in submission to Christ. He takes the things of Christ as they fall from His lips and conveys them with living power to the obedient soul. Thus we may take a perfect impress of the Author of truth (*In Heavenly Places,* p. 236).

## A deeper commitment

Something remarkable happened in the Upper Room. The Holy Spirit brought deep conviction to each of the praying disciples. In the light of Christ's eternal sacrifice on the cross, they recognized that their own commitment was superficial. They understood that God was calling for a much deeper consecration. They realized the shallowness of their own surrender to the cause of Christ. They opened their hearts to the fullness of the Holy Spirit's working and totally committed their lives to doing His will. God then had clear channels through which to pour His Holy Spirit. Such absolute surrender to God's will also prepares our hearts to receive the fullness of the outpouring of the Holy Spirit. The latter rain will be poured out on surrendered hearts.

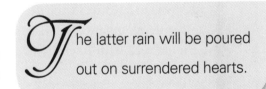

*The latter rain will be poured out on surrendered hearts.*

As you prayerfully reflect on the questions below, ask God to deepen your surrender.

1. Is the Holy Spirit convicting me to surrender anything in my life right now?
2. Is there something that I cherish that God may be calling me to surrender?
3. Read Psalm 51 in its entirety and ask God what He desires to teach you as you read. Meditate especially on the following verses from Psalm 51.

"Create in me a clean heart, O God, and renew a steadfast spirit within me. Do not cast me away from Your presence, and do not take Your Holy Spirit from me. Restore to me the joy of Your salvation, and uphold me with Your generous Spirit. Then I will teach transgressors Your ways and sinners will be converted to You" (Psalm 51:10–13).

## Section 2: Reflecting on Divine Counsel

Thoughtfully read the following excerpt from *Testimonies to Ministers,* pages 506–508.

"Ask ye of the Lord rain in the time of the latter rain; so the Lord shall make bright clouds, and give them showers of rain." "He will cause to come down for you the rain, the former rain, and the latter rain." In the East the former rain falls at the sowing time. It is necessary in order that the seed may germinate. Under the influence of the fertilizing showers, the tender shoot springs up. The latter rain, falling near the close of the season, ripens the grain and prepares it for the sickle. The Lord employs these operations of nature to represent the work of the Holy Spirit. As the dew and the rain are given first to cause the seed to germinate, and then to ripen the harvest, so the Holy Spirit is given to carry forward, from one stage to another, the process of spiritual growth. The ripening of the grain represents the completion of the work of God's grace in the soul. By the power of the Holy Spirit the moral image of God is to be perfected in the character. We are to be wholly transformed into the likeness of Christ.

> *The ripening of the grain represents the completion of the work of God's grace in the soul.*

The latter rain, ripening earth's harvest, represents the spiritual grace that prepares the church for the coming of the Son of man. But unless the former rain has fallen, there will be no life; the green blade will not spring up. Unless the early showers have done their work, the latter rain can bring no seed to perfection.

There is to be "first the blade, then the ear, after that the full corn in the ear." There must be a constant development of Christian virtue, a constant advancement in Christian experience. This we should seek with intensity of desire, that we may adorn the doctrine of Christ our Saviour.

**[page 507]**

Many have in a great measure failed to receive the former rain. They have not obtained all the benefits that God has thus provided for them. They expect that the lack will be supplied by the latter rain. When the richest abundance of grace shall be bestowed, they intend to open their hearts to receive it. They are making a terrible mistake. The work that God has begun in the human heart in giving His light and knowledge must be continually going forward. Every individual must realize his own necessity. The heart must be emptied of every defilement and cleansed for the indwelling of the Spirit. It was by the confession and forsaking of sin, by earnest prayer and consecration of themselves to God, that the early disciples prepared for the outpouring of the Holy Spirit on the Day of Pentecost. The same work, only in greater degree, must be done now.

> *The work that God has begun in the human heart in giving His light and knowledge must be continually going forward.*

## Day 8: Obedient Surrender

Then the human agent had only to ask for the blessing, and wait for the Lord to perfect the work concerning him. It is God who began the work, and He will finish His work, making man complete in Jesus Christ. But there must be no neglect of the grace represented by the former rain. Only those who are living up to the light they have will receive greater light. Unless we are daily advancing in the exemplification of the active Christian virtues, we shall not recognize the manifestations of the Holy Spirit in the latter rain. It may be falling on hearts all around us, but we shall not discern or receive it.

At no point in our experience can we dispense with the assistance of that which enables us to make the first start. The blessings received under the former rain are needful to us to the end. Yet these alone will not suffice. While we cherish the blessing of the early rain, we must not, on the other hand, lose sight of the **[page 508]** fact that without the latter rain, to fill out the ears and ripen the grain, the harvest will not be ready for the sickle, and the labor of the sower will have been in vain. Divine grace is needed at the beginning, divine grace at every step of advance, and divine grace alone can complete the work. There is no place for us to rest in a careless attitude. We must never forget the warnings of Christ, "Watch unto prayer," "Watch, . . . and pray always." A connection with the divine agency every moment is essential to our progress. We may have had a measure of the Spirit of God, but by prayer and faith we are continually to seek more of the Spirit. It will never do to cease our efforts. If we do not progress, if we do not place ourselves in an attitude to receive both the former and the latter rain, we shall lose our souls, and the responsibility will lie at our own door.

"Ask ye of the Lord rain in the time of the latter rain." Do not rest satisfied that in the ordinary course of the season, rain will fall. Ask for it. The growth and perfection of the seed rests not with the husbandman. God alone can ripen the harvest. But man's co-operation is required. God's work for us demands the action of our mind, the exercise of our faith. We must seek His favors with the whole heart if the showers of grace are to come to us. We should improve every opportunity of placing ourselves in the channel of blessing. Christ has said, "Where two or three are gathered together in My name, there am I in the midst." The convocations of the church, as in camp meetings, the assemblies of the home church, and all occasions where there is personal labor for souls, are God's appointed opportunities for giving the early and the latter rain.

# Section 3: Applying Divine Counsel
## Praying for the Latter Rain

If God is more willing to give us His Holy Spirit than a loving father is to give good gifts to His children, why is it necessary to pray for the Holy Spirit's descent upon us (Luke 11:13)? Is God reluctant to grant us His abundant blessing?

In today's lesson we will discover some answers to these vital questions.

1. What is the first major purpose of the latter rain? (See *Testimonies to Ministers,* page 506, paragraphs 1 and 2.)

   A. "By the power of the Holy Spirit _____

   _____

   _____

   _____."

   B. "The latter rain, ripening earth's harvest, represents the _____

   _____

   _____

   _____

   _____."

2. Why will many church members fail to receive the latter rain? (See *Testimonies to Ministers,* page 506, paragraph 2.)

   _____

   _____

   _____

   _____

3. How did the disciples prepare to receive the outpouring of the Holy Spirit on the Day of Pentecost? (See *Testimonies to Ministers,* page 507, paragraph 1.)

   A. "It was by the _____ and _____
   of sin, by earnest _____ and _____,
   of _____,
   that the early disciples prepared for the outpouring of the Holy Spirit on the Day of Pentecost."

4. Who will receive the outpouring of the Holy Spirit in the latter rain? (See *Testimonies to Ministers,* page 507, paragraph 1, last part.)

A. "Only those who are _____

_____

_____

_____."

B. "Unless we are _____

_____

_____

_____."

The early rain and latter rain work together from the start to the finish of the agricultural cycle. It takes both to produce the final harvest. The work of the Holy Spirit is similar. "Divine grace is needed at the beginning, divine grace at every step of advance, and divine grace alone can complete the work" (*Testimonies to Ministers,* page 508, paragraph 1).

5. What must we avoid at all costs in our Christian lives, and what must we daily seek? (See *Testimonies to Ministers,* page 508, paragraph 1.)

A. "There is no place for us to rest in a _____."

B. "We may have had a measure of the Spirit of God, but _____

_____."

C. "If we do not progress, if _____

_____

_____."

The problem is not with God. He is more than willing to pour out His Holy Spirit on our thirsty souls. The problem is we are not ready to receive the fullness of God's blessing. Heaven's urgent appeal to God's end-time people is to prepare to receive the latter rain. He is calling us to prayer, repentance, confession, humility, and commitment. Will you bow your head right now and tell God you desire to make seeking the power of His Spirit a priority in your life?

# Day 9

# Joyful Thanksgiving

The Holy Spirit filled the hearts of the disciples with joyful praise. They no longer faced the future with fear, so their confidence soared. Their Savior had forgiven their sins. Their guilt was gone. Their lives were transformed by the power of the Spirit. Their best Friend was at the right hand of God's throne to supply all their needs. Now they had something to sing about. Their lives overflowed with thanksgiving to the Christ, who had redeemed them. Luke records this joyful expression of thanksgiving and praise in these words: "Continuing daily with one accord in the temple, and breaking bread from house to house, they ate their food with gladness and simplicity of heart, praising God and having favor with all the people. And the Lord added to the church daily those who were being saved" (Acts 2:46, 47).

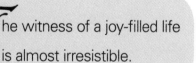

The witness of a joy-filled life is almost irresistible.

The disciples were awestruck with wonder. Joy overflowed from hearts filled with gratitude.

The testimony of the lame man healed through the power of Christ by Peter at the temple gate reveals this praise overflowing from a grateful heart. As new strength flowed into the lame man's ankles and legs, the Scripture records, "He, leaping up, stood and walked and entered the temple with them—walking, leaping, and praising God. And all the people saw him walking and praising God" (Acts 3:8, 9). Christ had so remarkably transformed this man's life that the only logical response was praise and thanksgiving. His testimony sprang from a heart full of gratitude. He could not hide his appreciation for the One who had done so much for him.

# Day 9: Joyful Thanksgiving

## Transformed in the Upper Room

The disciples experienced a transformation in the Upper Room, and their hearts were filled with gratitude too. Like this lame man, they experienced the power of the living Christ in their own lives. They realized the magnitude of what the Savior had done for them on the cross. They understood more deeply the significance of His overwhelming sacrifice. Describing this Upper Room experience, Ellen White affirms,

> The Spirit came upon the waiting, praying disciples with a fullness that reached every heart. The Infinite One revealed Himself in power to His church. It was as if for ages this influence had been held in restraint, and now Heaven rejoiced in being able to pour out upon the church the riches of the Spirit's grace. And under the influence of the Spirit, words of penitence and confession mingled with songs of praise for sins forgiven. Words of thanksgiving and of prophecy were heard. All heaven bent low to behold and to adore the wisdom of matchless, incomprehensible love. Lost in wonder, the apostles exclaimed, "Herein is love." They grasped the imparted gift. And what followed? The sword of the Spirit, newly edged with power and bathed in the lightnings of heaven, cut its way through unbelief. Thousands were converted in a day (*The Acts of the Apostles*, p. 38).

The disciples never tired of telling the story of Jesus' love. They were eternally grateful for His sacrifice. Even in the most difficult periods of their lives, they recounted the magnificence of the gift of salvation. This is why they could sing in suffering, rejoice while being persecuted, and praise while imprisoned. Imagine the Philippian jailer's response when he heard Paul and Silas, at midnight, praying and singing hymns to God. Bound in chains, imprisoned in a dark, dismal prison, they rejoiced in the goodness of God. This evidently made an impression on the prisoners because the record states that "the prisoners were listening to them" (Acts 16:25). The jailer was impressed with their faith as well. When an earthquake totally destroyed the prison, the jailer expected that the prisoners already would have fled, likely requiring him to pay for their escape with his life. He was shocked to discover Paul and Silas still there, along with every one of the other prisoners. Overwhelmed with the godliness of these two followers of Jesus, the jailer surrendered his life to Christ. There is something powerful about a life overflowing with joy, thanksgiving, and praise. Joy is one of the fruits of the Spirit. Thanksgiving and praise flow from a heart filled with joy.

> Even in the most difficult periods of their lives, they recounted the magnificence of the gift of salvation.

## The joy of Jesus

The witness of a joy-filled life is almost irresistible. Skeptical people are more interested in seeing a demonstration of the gospel lived out in a life filled with joy than in listening to a sermon. The fundamental question that each professing Christian must ask is, Does my attitude reveal the joy of Jesus to the people around me? Do they see praise and thanksgiving reflected in my life? The New Testament believers radiated the joy of Jesus.

Writing to the church at Philippi, the apostle Paul instructed, "Rejoice in the Lord always. Again I will say, rejoice!" (Philippians 4:4). He suggested that the Ephesians express their joy by "speaking to one another in psalms and hymns and spiritual songs, singing and making melody in your heart to the Lord, giving thanks always for all things to God the Father in the name of our Lord Jesus Christ" (Ephesians 5:19). The apostle admonished the Colossians to "continue earnestly in prayer, being vigilant in it with thanksgiving" (Colossians 4:2). These newly converted Christians changed the world not only by what they taught but because of how they lived. Their godly words were matched by godly lives.

Their thankfulness was not dependent on everything always going right in their lives. They did not praise God just when they were prosperous and healthy. They praised at all times because, even in the worst of times, they had something to praise about. I am reminded of Matthew Henry, the nineteenth-century English preacher, who was robbed one day. That evening he wrote in his diary, "I was robbed today and I thank Thee first because I was never robbed before; second, because although they took my purse they did not take my life; third, because although they took my all, it was not much; and fourth because it was I who was robbed, and not I who robbed."

> When we complain about the circumstances of life, we actually charge God with being unjust.

What a testimony. When we complain about the circumstances of life, we actually charge God with being unjust. Trust during life's difficult times reveals confidence in a God who is in control of the universe and is actively guiding our lives. Many things that happen to us are unfair and downright wrong. But even in these, the most painful and hurtful experiences, we can rejoice in a Savior whose love will never let us go and who will one day make all wrongs right. God will pour out His Holy Spirit in latter-rain power on those who have discovered the secret of trust even in life's most difficult times. If we discover how to praise Him in the darkness, we will receive the morning showers of the latter rain. If we can sing in the dark, we will experience the refreshing of a new day in the fullness of the Spirit's power.

When we are charmed by His grace, amazed at His love, and overwhelmed with His goodness, there will be no experience in our lives that can destroy the inner joy and peace He gives. We may experience pain, but deep within there is a reservoir of joy that buoys us up. We may go through heartache, but rivers of joy flood our souls. What He has done for us, what He is doing for us, and what He will do for us keep us joyful in life's storms.

In the Upper Room, the disciples opened their hearts to His overwhelming joy. Their hearts were filled with thanksgiving and praise.

Prayerfully reflect on the questions below.

1. Has anything in your life robbed you of the joy Jesus longs for you to have? Why?
2. Spend a few moments considering all you have in Christ. What are His greatest gifts to you?
3. Do others around you see His joy reflected in your life?
4. Are joy, thanksgiving, and praise feelings or choices?
5. How can you choose to be thankful even when you do not feel thankful?

# Section 2: Reflecting on Divine Counsel

Thoughtfully read the following excerpt from *Testimonies to Ministers,* pages 509–512.

The circumstances may seem to be favorable for a rich outpouring of the showers of grace. But God Himself must command the rain to fall. Therefore we should not be remiss in supplication. We are not to trust to the ordinary working of providence. We must pray that God will unseal the fountain of the water of life. And we must ourselves receive of the living water. Let us, with contrite hearts, pray most earnestly that now, in the time of the latter rain, the showers of grace may fall upon us. At every meeting we attend our prayers should ascend, that at this very time God will impart warmth and moisture to our souls. As we seek God for the Holy Spirit, it will work in us meekness, humbleness of mind, a conscious dependence upon God for the perfecting latter rain. If we pray for the blessing in faith, we shall receive it as God has promised.

> If we pray for the blessing in faith, we shall receive it as God has promised.

The continued communication of the Holy Spirit to the church is represented by the prophet Zechariah under another figure, which contains a wonderful lesson of encouragement for us. The prophet says: "The angel that talked with me came again, and waked me, as a man that is wakened out of his sleep, and said unto me, What seest thou? And I said, I have looked, and behold a candlestick all of gold, with a bowl upon the top of it, and his seven lamps thereon, and seven pipes to the seven lamps, which are upon the top thereof: and two olive trees by it, one upon the right side of the bowl, and the other upon the left side thereof. So I answered and spake to the angel that talked with me, saying, What are these, my lord? . . . Then he answered and spake unto me, saying, This **[page 510]** is the word of the Lord unto Zerubbabel, saying, Not by might, nor by power, but by My Spirit, saith the Lord of hosts. . . . And I answered again, and said unto him, What be these two olive branches which through the two golden pipes empty the golden oil out of themselves? . . . Then said he, These are the two anointed ones, that stand by the Lord of the whole earth."

From the two olive trees, the golden oil was emptied through golden pipes into the bowl of the candlestick and thence into the golden lamps that gave light to the sanctuary. So from the holy ones that stand in God's presence, His Spirit is imparted to human instrumentalities that are consecrated to His service. The mission of the two anointed ones is to communicate light and power to God's people. It is to receive blessing for us that they stand in God's presence. As the olive trees empty themselves into the golden pipes, so the heavenly messengers seek to communicate all that they receive from God. The whole heavenly treasure

> So from the holy ones that stand in God's presence, His Spirit is imparted to human instrumentalities that are consecrated to His service.

awaits our demand and reception; and as we receive the blessing, we in our turn are to impart it. Thus it is that the holy lamps are fed, and the church becomes a light bearer in the world.

> *We should daily receive the holy oil, that we may impart to others. All may be light bearers to the world if they will.*

This is the work that the Lord would have every soul prepared to do at this time, when the four angels are holding the four winds, that they shall not blow until the servants of God are sealed in their foreheads. There is no time now for self-pleasing. The lamps of the soul must be trimmed. They must be supplied with the oil of grace. Every precaution must be taken to prevent spiritual declension, lest the great day of the Lord overtake us as a thief in the night. Every witness for God is now to work intelligently in the lines which **[page 511]** God has appointed. We should daily obtain a deep and living experience in the work of perfecting Christian character. We should daily receive the holy oil, that we may impart to others. All may be light bearers to the world if they will. We are to sink self out of sight in Jesus. We are to receive the word of the Lord in counsel and instruction, and gladly communicate it. There is now need of much prayer. Christ commands, "Pray without ceasing;" that is, keep the mind uplifted to God, the source of all power and efficiency.

We may have long followed the narrow path, but it is not safe to take this as proof that we shall follow it to the end. If we have walked with God in fellowship of the Spirit, it is because we have sought Him daily by faith. From the two olive trees the golden oil flowing through the golden pipes has been communicated to us. But those who do not cultivate the spirit and habit of prayer cannot expect to receive the golden oil of goodness, patience, long-suffering, gentleness, love.

> *Everyone is to keep himself separate from the world, which is full of iniquity.*

Everyone is to keep himself separate from the world, which is full of iniquity. We are not to walk with God for a time, and then part from His company and walk in the sparks of our own kindling. There must be a firm continuance, a perseverance in acts of faith. We are to praise God; to show forth His glory in a righteous character. No one of us will gain the victory without persevering, untiring effort, proportionate to the value of the object which we seek, even eternal life.

The dispensation in which we are now living is to be, to those that ask, the dispensation of the Holy Spirit. Ask for His blessing. It is time we were more intense in our devotion. To us is committed the arduous, but happy, glorious work of revealing Christ to those who are in darkness. We are called to proclaim the special **[page 512]** truths for this time. For all this the outpouring of the Spirit is essential. We should pray for it. The Lord expects us to ask Him. We have not been wholehearted in this work.

# Section 3: Applying Divine Counsel
## Revealing the Fruits of the Spirit

As we seek the infilling of the Holy Spirit and open our hearts to receive the heavenly Guest, He will make a dramatic difference in our lives. The reception of the Holy Spirit produces the fruits of the Spirit. If the fruits of the Spirit are not manifested in our daily interactions with one another, there is no genuine evidence that we are filled with the Spirit. When the Holy Spirit is poured out, He makes a difference in how we think, live, and relate to others. In this lesson we will study how the Holy Spirit works to transform our characters and produce the fruits of the Spirit in our lives.

1. The fruits of the Holy Spirit are listed in Galatians 5:22, 23. Read each of the fruits of the Spirit listed below and write a one-sentence definition or description of that particular fruit of the Spirit. What do these fruits mean to you?

A. Love _____

_____

_____

B. Joy _____

_____

_____

C. Peace _____

_____

_____

D. Long-suffering _____

_____

_____

E. Kindness _____

_____

_____

F. Goodness _____

_____

_____

G. Faithfulness _____

_____

_____

H. Gentleness _____

_____

_____

I. Self-control _____

_____

_____

2. Which three of these spiritual fruits do you regularly manifest in your life?

A. _____

B. _____

C. _____

3. Which three of these spiritual fruits would you like to manifest more?

A. _____

B. _____

C. _____

4. What three specific attitudes will the Holy Spirit "work within us" as we pray for the latter rain? (See *Testimonies to Ministers,* page 509.)

As we seek God, the Holy Spirit will work in us:

A. _____

B. _____

C. _____

5. "Christ commands, 'Pray without ceasing;' that is, to keep the mind uplifted to God, the source of all power and efficiency" (*Testimonies to Ministers,* p. 511). What is the result of a careless, complacent attitude toward seeking God in prayer? (See *Testimonies to Ministers,* page 511.)

# Day 9: Joyful Thanksgiving

"Those who do not cultivate the spirit and habit of prayer . . .

_____

_____."

The Holy Spirit, the Third Person of the Godhead, is Heaven's life-transforming Agent. He alone can provide us with the spiritual power to make a difference in our lives. Deeply entrenched habit patterns can be transformed only by the Holy Spirit. Sins deeply embedded in our characters can be overcome only by the power of the Holy Spirit. Self-centered dispositional traits and attitudes can be changed only by the Holy Spirit.

Allowing the Holy Spirit to powerfully reveal Jesus' love and grace through their lives is the priority of all Christians. Jesus summarizes it this way: "Seek first the kingdom of God and His righteousness, and all these things shall be added to you" (Matthew 6:33). As we seek God alone in prayer, the Holy Spirit will enter our hearts and change our lives.

- "There is now need of much prayer" (*Testimonies to Ministers,* p. 511).
- "A revival need be expected only in answer to prayer" (*Selected Messages,* bk. 1, p. 121).

Will you open your heart to God and plead for the outpouring of the Holy Spirit today? Will you ask Him to reveal the fruits of the Spirit in your life?

Are you willing to surrender everything not in harmony with His will?

Why not pray this prayer today:

*Dear Lord,*

*I humbly acknowledge that I do not always reveal the fruits of the Spirit in my life. At times I am not patient, kind, and gentle. Sometimes I do not exhibit the grace of self-control. Today, I sincerely repent of my lack. I confess my sins and open my heart to You. I believe You can do more for me through Your Holy Spirit than I can ever do myself. I give You permission right now to transform my life to reveal the fruits of the Spirit and manifest Your loving character.*

*In Jesus' name, amen.*

# Day 10

# Passionate Witness

Imagine the disciples' reaction to the Great Commission. The task seemed overwhelming. The mandate to take the gospel to the entire world seemed impossible. How could such a small group of disciples make any significant impact on the mighty Roman Empire? First-century Roman society was dominated by political intrigue, rampant materialism, self-centered pride, all-consuming greed, blatant immorality, and religious superstition. Steeped in millennia of tradition, Jerusalem did not appear to be a fertile territory for the prospect of the gospel either. These early followers of Christ must have wondered if Jesus' command to "go into all the world and preach the gospel to every creature" was even remotely possible (Mark 16:15).

> As the disciples proclaimed the message of redeeming grace, hearts yielded to the power of this message. The church beheld converts flocking to her from all directions.

## The Great Commission and the great promise

Fortunately, the Great Commission was accompanied by a great promise. Jesus said, "All authority has been given to Me in heaven and on earth. Go therefore and make disciples of all the nations" (Matthew 28:18, 19). He then added, "You shall receive power when the Holy Spirit is come upon you; and you shall be witnesses to Me in Jerusalem, and in all Judea and Samaria, and to the end of the earth"

# Day 10: Passionate Witness

(Acts 1:8). The Great Commission was to be accomplished only in His power. The disciples were to witness in His strength—not in their own. They were to go forth filled with the Spirit, empowered by the Spirit, and guided by the Spirit. It would be the Holy Spirit's presence and power in their lives that would give them success.

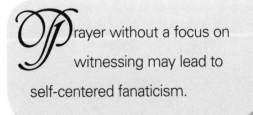
Prayer without a focus on witnessing may lead to self-centered fanaticism.

What was the result of the outpouring of the Spirit on the Day of Pentecost? The glad tidings of a risen Saviour were carried to the uttermost parts of the inhabited world. As the disciples proclaimed the message of redeeming grace, hearts yielded to the power of this message. The church beheld converts flocking to her from all directions. Backsliders were reconverted. Sinners united with believers in seeking the pearl of great price. Some who had been the bitterest opponents of the gospel became its champions. The prophecy was fulfilled, "He that is feeble . . . shall be as David; and the house of David . . . as the angel of the Lord." Zechariah 12:8. Every Christian saw in his brother a revelation of divine love and benevolence. One interest prevailed; one subject of emulation swallowed up all others. The ambition of the believers was to reveal the likeness of Christ's character and to labor for the enlargement of His kingdom (*The Acts of the Apostles,* p. 48).

The Holy Spirit's power was poured out on the Day of Pentecost to enable the disciples to carry the gospel to the world. The Holy Spirit empowered the witness of these disciples, and the results were remarkable: Hearts were touched. Lives were changed. Three thousand were baptized in just one day. This evangelistic momentum continued, and thousands more were added to the church in a few short years. Acts 4:4 records, "Many of those who heard the word believed; and the number of the men came to be about five thousand." Acts 6:7 states, "The word of God spread, and the number of the disciples multiplied greatly." According to Acts 9:31, new churches were planted in Judea, Galilee, and Samaria and they "multiplied." The gospel penetrated cultural, national, and linguistic barriers. Peter was miraculously led to witness to Cornelius, an Italian centurion seeking for truth; and Philip explained the mysteries of the Cross to an influential Ethiopian. The biblical book we call The Acts of the Apostles might have been more accurately titled The Acts of the Holy Spirit.

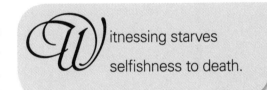
Witnessing starves selfishness to death.

## Witnessing: The purpose of the outpouring of the Spirit

When the church has little interest in witnessing, there is little evidence of the Holy Spirit. Why would God pour out His Spirit in the fullness of power to witness if His people had little interest in witnessing? The power of the Holy Spirit is not an end in itself. The promised latter rain is to accomplish the mission of taking the gospel to the world. Prayer without a focus on witnessing may lead to self-centered fanaticism. Bible study without witness can lead to self-righteous formalism. The Pharisees prayed and studied the Scriptures for hours each day, but they condemned Jesus to death. Why? There is one simple reason. Their self-centered lives had little room for a selfless Messiah.

In contrast, witnessing starves selfishness to death. Heartfelt prayer, earnest Bible study, and passionate witness are the keys of all genuine revivals. The fundamental purpose of prayer and Bible study is to draw us close to Jesus so He can trust us with the outpouring of the Holy Spirit's power in mighty witness. The latter rain will not be poured out to glorify our egos. It will not be unleashed to transform complacent church members to become passionate witnesses. It is the work of the early rain of the Spirit to convict us of sin, to empower us to face the enemy, and to reorder our priorities for witnessing. The latter rain falls to complete the work of God's grace in our lives and in the world. We are counseled that

unless the members of God's church today have a living connection with the Source of all spiritual growth, they will not be ready for the time of reaping. Unless they keep their lamps trimmed and burning, they will fail of receiving added grace in times of special need.

Those only who are constantly receiving fresh supplies of grace, will have power proportionate to their daily need and their ability to use that power. Instead of looking forward to some future time when, through a special endowment of spiritual power, they will receive a miraculous fitting up for soul winning, they are yielding themselves daily to God, that He may make them vessels meet for His use. Daily they are improving the opportunities for service that lie within their reach. Daily they are witnessing for the Master wherever they may be, whether in some humble sphere of labor in the home, or in a public field of usefulness (*The Acts of the Apostles,* p. 55).

In the Upper Room, the disciples committed themselves to take the gospel to the world. Their personal agendas were laid aside to accomplish Christ's agenda. Their personal plans were surrendered to accomplish Christ's great plan. Their human ambitions were left behind so they could move forward with Christ's one ambition to redeem the human race. They were passionate about sharing with the world the news about Christ, who had transformed their lives.

One desire swallowed up all others—to fulfill Christ's commission and proclaim the gospel to the world.

> The Holy Spirit will be poured out in latter-rain power on those who are witnessing for Jesus so that God's work on earth can be finished and we can go home.

What is your chief desire in life? Do you long for the power of the Holy Spirit to empower your witness? Are you regularly sharing your faith with others? If you were condemned in a court of law for sharing your faith with others and witnessing about the good news of Jesus, would there be enough evidence to convict you? The Holy Spirit will be poured out in latter-rain power on those who are witnessing for Jesus so that God's work on earth can be finished and we can go home. Would you like to reorder the priorities in your life and make a commitment to be a more faithful witness for Jesus? Are you willing to allow the Holy Spirit to use you in whatever ways He desires you to witness for Him? Will you lay aside your own personal agenda and commit your life to the one thing that will really matter in the end, winning the lost for Jesus? Our life circumstances are different. Our family and work responsibilities vary. Everyone cannot do the same thing. Simply tell God you long to share His love with others and allow Him to guide you.

# Section 2: Reflecting on Divine Counsel
## All Other Blessings

Thoughtfully read the following excerpts from *Testimonies to Ministers,* pages 511, 512, and 174–176.

The dispensation in which we are now living is to be, to those that ask, the dispensation of the Holy Spirit. Ask for His blessing. It is time we were more intense in our devotion. To us is committed the arduous, but happy, glorious work of revealing Christ to those who are in darkness. We are called to proclaim the special **[page 512]** truths for this time. For all this the outpouring of the Spirit is essential. We should pray for it. The Lord expects us to ask Him. We have not been wholehearted in this work.

> *P*ray without ceasing, and watch by working in accordance with your prayers.

What can I say to my brethren in the name of the Lord? What proportion of our efforts has been made in accordance with the light the Lord has been pleased to give? We cannot depend upon form or external machinery. What we need is the quickening influence of the Holy Spirit of God. "Not by might, nor by power, but by My Spirit, saith the Lord of hosts." Pray without ceasing, and watch by working in accordance with your prayers. As you pray, believe, trust in God. It is the time of the latter rain, when the Lord will give largely of His Spirit. Be fervent in prayer, and watch in the Spirit.

* * * * *

This promised blessing [the Holy Spirit], if claimed by faith, would **[page 175]** bring all other blessings in its train, and it is to be given liberally to the people of God. Through the cunning devices of the enemy the minds of God's people seem to be incapable of comprehending and appropriating the promises of God. They seem to think that only the scantiest showers of grace are to fall upon the thirsty soul. The people of God have accustomed themselves to think that they must rely upon their own efforts, that little help is to be received from heaven; and the result is that they have little light to communicate to other souls who are dying in error and darkness. The church has long been contented with little of the blessing of God; they have not felt the need

> *T*he church has long been contented with little of the blessing of God.

of reaching up to the exalted privileges purchased for them at infinite cost. Their spiritual strength has been feeble, their experience of a dwarfed and crippled character, and they are disqualified for the work the Lord would have them to do. They are not able to present the great and glorious truths of God's Holy Word that would convict and convert souls through the agency of the Holy Spirit. The power of God awaits their demand and reception. A harvest of joy will be reaped by those who sow the holy seeds of truth. "He that goeth forth and weepeth, bearing precious seed, shall doubtless come again with rejoicing, bringing his sheaves with him."

The world have received the idea from the attitude of the church that God's people are indeed a joyless people, that the service of Christ is unattractive, that the blessing of God is bestowed at severe cost to the receivers. By dwelling upon our trials, and making much of difficulties, we misrepresent God and Jesus Christ whom He has sent; for the path to heaven is made unattractive by the gloom that gathers about the soul of the believer, and many turn in disappointment from the service of Christ. But are those who [page 176] thus present Christ believers? No, for believers rely upon the divine promise, and the Holy Spirit is a comforter as well as a reprover.

> A harvest of joy will be reaped by those who sow the holy seeds of truth.

The Christian must build all the foundation if he would build a strong, symmetrical character, if he would be well balanced in his religious experience. It is in this way that the man will be prepared to meet the demands of truth and righteousness as they are represented in the Bible; for he will be sustained and energized by the Holy Spirit of God. He who is a true Christian combines great tenderness of feeling with great firmness of purpose, with unswerving fidelity to God; he will in no case become the betrayer of sacred trusts. He who is endowed with the Holy Spirit has great capacities of heart and intellect, with strength of will and purpose that is unconquerable.

# Section 3: Applying Divine Counsel
## Accepting the Promise

Is the reception of the latter rain a future event solely determined by God? Is the outpouring of the Holy Spirit in end-time power something we are to idly wait for until the right time arrives? Is God waiting to pour out His Holy Spirit at a certain time in the future when prophetic events unfold?

In today's lesson we will study the divine counsel about the timing of the outpouring of the Holy Spirit!

1. What specific counsel regarding the latter rain do the Old Testament prophets Zechariah and Hosea give us? (See Zechariah 10:1; Hosea 10:12.) _____

   _____

   _____

2. When is the time of the latter rain? (See *Testimonies to Ministers,* pages 511, 512.)

   A. "The dispensation of in which we are now living is to be, to those that ask,

   _____

   _____

   _____

   Ask for His blessing. It is time we were more intense in our devotion."

   B. "It is the _____

   _____

   _____."

Many church members are looking forward to a future date for the outpouring of the Holy Spirit, but God promises we can have it now.

3. What impression regarding the Holy Spirit is often given? (See *Testimonies to Ministers,* page 174.)

   "Other blessings and privileges have been set before the people until a desire has been awakened in the church for the attainment of the blessing promised of God; but

   _____

   _____

   _____."

4. What is the result of the lack of fullness of the Holy Spirit's power? Read *Testimonies to Ministers,* pages 174 and 175, under the heading "All Other Blessings." Then list the blessings our Lord so freely offers in the latter rain.

A. "God's people seem to be incapable of _____

_____

_____."

B. "The people of God have accustomed themselves to _____

_____

_____."

C. "Their spiritual strength has been _____

_____

_____."

D. "They are disqualified _____

_____

_____."

E. "They are not able to _____

_____

_____."

Look at each lack listed above and turn it into a positive. What will the outpouring of the Holy Spirit bring to our lives that is the exact opposite of items listed in "A to E" above?

A.                                              D.


B.                                              E.


C.


5. What promise does our Lord make to us about the outpouring of the Holy Spirit? (See *Testimonies to Ministers,* page 175.)

# Day 10: Passionate Witness

"The power of God _____

_____

_____."

    All of Heaven longs to pour out the latter rain. As we seek God in humility, confessing our sins, humbling our hearts, surrendering our lives to His purposes, He will move powerfully. He will do for us what we could never do for ourselves. His love will be revealed to the world. His grace will change lives. Multitudes will rejoice in His truth. The work of God on earth will soon be finished, and Jesus will come.

## Seeking a deeper experience

    Do you long for a deeper experience with God? Do you sense the need for the mighty working of the Holy Spirit in your own life? Would you like to participate with Christ in the closing work of this earth's history? Do you desire to receive the outpouring of the Holy Spirit in the latter rain for the finishing of God's work on earth?

    In the ten chapters of this workbook, we have studied how to prepare for the reception of the Holy Spirit in latter-rain power. The Holy Spirit has moved upon our hearts. We have sensed His presence. He has led us to a deeper surrender. Habits and attitudes that we were unaware of have surfaced. Long-cherished sins have been forsaken. We have knelt before our Lord, confessing and repenting for the times we have disappointed Him. In unity we have sought Him in prayer with fellow Christians, and we have come from these periods of intercession spiritually renewed.

    You may be wondering, "How can I sustain this new experience? Are there some specific things I can now do to maintain this deeper relationship with God?" Fortunately there are. In the days ahead, you can do three specific things to keep growing in Jesus.

1. Set aside specific times each day for prayer. As you kneel before His throne, Jesus will impart His Spirit to you daily. Claim His promise in Luke 11:13, "If you then being evil, know how to give good gifts to your children, how much more will Your heavenly Father give the Holy Spirit to those who ask Him!" Choose a prayer partner or join a prayer group and set aside a time to meet weekly. These prayer sessions will become an anchor of your faith.

2. Commit to spend time each day in studying His Word. The Holy Spirit fills our lives as we fill our minds with the Word of God. We are changed, transformed, and renewed through the Word of God. The apostle Peter, who had experienced the life-changing power of Pentecost, reminded fellow Christians that they had been given "exceedingly great and precious promises, that through these you may be partakers of the divine nature, having escaped the corruption that is in the world through lust" (2 Peter 1:4). You may desire to focus on the life of Jesus and meditate on His life as recorded in the Gospels. You will find yourself inspired by His love and led deeper in your Christian walk of faith. Personal, devotional Bible study is the basis for all genuine spiritual growth.

3. Make witnessing a part of your daily life. Look for opportunities to share your faith daily. Witnessing Christians are growing Christians. Become involved in some area of service in your local church. Because "it is more blessed to give than to receive" (Acts 20:35), as we share Jesus' love with others, we are the ones most blessed. Witnessing starves selfishness to death. It leads us to a deeper dependence on God. It drives us to our knees to seek His power, and it leads us back to the Bible to find answers to the questions others are asking. On Pentecost, the purpose of Jesus' promise was to empower the disciples to take the gospel to the first-century world. The purpose of the outpouring of the Spirit in the final generation is to empower His people to complete the task. It is to finish His work. It is to empower His church to witness.

Would you like to be part of something great for God? Would you like to join a growing number of fellow church members who are seeking Him in prayer, placing priority on studying His Word, and witnessing for His kingdom?

If this is your desire, will you bow your head right now and make this commitment? As you do, our Lord will answer from heaven and move in your life in powerful ways. I pray that the Holy Spirit will fill your life and that you will be God's ambassador for revival in your family, your local church, and your community.

# Notes

# *Notes*